THE HEADINGLEY LECTURES

THE DOCTRINE OF
THE HOLY SPIRIT

★ *Contributors to this book*

VINCENT TAYLOR, Ph.D., D.D. (Lond.),
Principal and Professor of New Testament Language and Literature

HOWARD WATKIN-JONES, M.A., D.D. (Cantab),
Professor of Church History and History of Doctrine

HAROLD ROBERTS, M.A. (Wales), Ph.D. (Cantab),
Professor of Systematic Theology and Philosophy of Religion

NORMAN H. SNAITH, M.A. (Oxon),
Professor of Old Testament Languages and Literature

THE DOCTRINE OF
THE HOLY SPIRIT

Four Lectures
by
Members of the Staff
of Wesley College, Headingley

✶

WIPF & STOCK · Eugene, Oregon

Wipf and Stock Publishers
199 W 8th Ave, Suite 3
Eugene, OR 97401

The Doctrine of the Holy Spirit
Four Lectures by Members of the Staff of Wesley College, Headingly
By Taylor, Vincent and Watkin-Jones, Howard
Copyright©1937 Methodist Publishing - Epworth Press
ISBN 13: 978-1-4982-0496-5
Publication date 9/11/2014
Previously published by Epworth Press, 1937

Every effort has been made to trace the current copyright owner
of this publication but without success. If you have any information
or interest in the copyright, please contact the publishers.

CONTENTS

Lecture I

THE SPIRIT OF GOD IN JEWISH THOUGHT 9
By NORMAN H. SNAITH, M.A.

Lecture II

THE SPIRIT IN THE NEW TESTAMENT 39
By VINCENT TAYLOR, PH.D., D.D.

Lecture III

THE HOLY SPIRIT IN THE CHURCH 69
By HOWARD WATKIN-JONES, M.A., D.D.

Lecture IV

THE HOLY SPIRIT AND THE TRINITY 105
By HAROLD ROBERTS, M.A., PH.D.

PREFACE

THE FOLLOWING LECTURES were given by the members of the Staff of Wesley College, Headingley, Leeds, on successive days from June 8 to June 11, 1937, to the students of the College and to a number of Methodist ministers of the Leeds District. Each Lecture was followed by questions and discussion, and, in view of the interest created, it has been thought well to publish the four manuscripts in the hope that they may prove to be of use to a wider circle of readers. The Lectures are published substantially as they were delivered. Although prepared independently, they form, we believe, a unity in which the biblical foundations of the doctrine, its history in the life and thought of the Church, and its theological implications are successively set forth in outline.

I

THE SPIRIT OF GOD IN JEWISH THOUGHT

by

NORMAN H. SNAITH, M.A.

I

THE SPIRIT OF GOD IN JEWISH THOUGHT

(a) *The Spirit of God in the Old Testament*

IN THE OLD TESTAMENT, spirit [*ruach*] is fundamentally an activity of God. The word 'activity' is used designedly, and in preference to such words as 'characteristic' and 'attribute'. The God of the Old Testament is not 'One Who Is', so much as 'One Who Does', and the essential activeness of God is nowhere more clear than in this idea of the Spirit of the Lord [*ruach-adonai*]. The *ruach-adonai* is the manifestation in human experience of the life-giving, energy-creating power of God. Almost without exception, it is His power in and through the lives of men. Because of it, men are able to do those things which, of themselves and in their own strength, they are incapable of doing. The exceptions, the rare occasions when the *ruach-adonai* is spoken of apart from its action definitely in and through the lives of men, together with all those instances where the word *ruach* is used of men in what we, with our modern categories, would call a psychological sense, are to be explained either on the basis of the equation of breath and life, or by the association of the spirit and the wind. In any case, the association of *ruach* with life and power is firm and universal; and so also is the assumption that both life and power have their home in God, and always they belong to Him. The *ruach-adonai* is a gift to man direct from God. The *ruach* of man, whether used of his actual breath, of his stronger, more violent emotions, or even of his 'soul', is also of God. No man of himself has *ruach*, but only as it descends upon him from God, or is implanted in him by God. It comes to man from above, from outside.

1. THE 'RUACH-ADONAI' IS THE POWER OF GOD IN AND THROUGH THE LIVES OF MEN

The *ruach-adonai* is that power of God, descending upon men, by which they are enabled to do that which, in ordinary circumstances, is impossible. It is doubtful to what extent it is correct even to say 'they are enabled'. Rather it is God who works. This is always implicit, and is sometimes stated explicitly. It was not, for instance, Othniel son of Kenaz who saved Israel. That, of himself, neither he nor any mortal man could ever do, for salvation is of God alone. 'The *ruach-adonai* came upon him, and he judged Israel, and the Lord delivered Cushan-rishathaim king of

Mesopotamia into his hand; and his hand prevailed . . . ' (Judges iii. 10). Even more clearly, 'the *ruach-adonai* clothed itself with Gideon' (Judges vi. 34, R.V. marg.), or with Amasai (1 Chron. xii. 18). Cf. Judges xi. 29, xv. 18. When David was anointed by Samuel, 'the *ruach-adonai* came mightily upon David from that time forth' (1 Sam. xvi. 13). The next verse begins, 'Now the *ruach-adonai* had departed from Saul'. The inference is, as above, of Othniel son of Kenaz and his ability to judge Israel, that it was the *ruach-adonai* which made both Saul and David in turn capable of exercising kingly functions, and that, without the *ruach-adonai*, neither was 'sufficient for these things'. To slay a lion 'with nothing in his hand' is a feat expected not even of the strongest, but Samson so slew the lion 'when the *ruach-adonai* came mightily upon him' (Judges xiv. 6). Cf. Judges xiv. 19, xv. 14. Not only is all this true of physical strength and ability to rule; it holds also of other outstanding accomplishments. When Pharaoh exclaims, 'Can we find such an one as this, a man in whom the spirit of God [*ruach-elohim*] rests?' (Gen. xli. 38; E, not J), it is in the belief that 'interpretations belong to God' (Gen. xl. 8; cf. xli. 16). This skill to interpret dreams is ascribed to God, not only in the early Elohist tradition, but also in the late Daniel, where it is said, 'There is a God in heaven that revealeth secrets' (ii. 28). In a similar way the Lord called Bezalel the son of Uri, and 'filled him with the *ruach-elohim*, in wisdom, and in understanding, and in knowledge, and in all manner of workmanship' (Exod. xxxi. 3, xxxv. 31; P), in order that he might be able to make all the furniture of the Tent.

In the earliest records, possession by the *ruach-adonai* is scarcely to be differentiated by us from demonic possession. In the time of Saul, for instance, there were companies of prophets parading the countryside, uttering weird cries and exhibiting a strange and contagious frenzy. This excitement, neither ethical nor religious in our use of the terms, is ascribed to possession by the *ruach-adonai* (1 Sam. x. 6, 10, xix. 20, 23), indistinguishable as it is from the habit of dancing dervishes or the custom of native witch-doctors. Compare 2 Kings iii. 15, where Elisha calls for a minstrel, and 'when the minstrel played, the hand of the Lord came upon him'. The ancient association of minstrelsy and prophecy is seen, somewhat surprisingly, in 1 Chron. xxv. 1–3, where the sons of Asaph, Heman, and Jeduthun, the official musicians and singers of the Second Temple, are said to 'prophesy with harps, with psalteries, and with cymbals'. All strange behaviour, however strange, was, in the earlier days of the kingdom, regarded as being due to the *ruach-adonai.* In fact, the stranger the behaviour, the more definite was the ascription. Jehovah had everything to do with it. Volz (*Der Geist Gottes*, 1910, p. 5) postulates a '*ruach*-demon', with which originally Jehovah has nothing whatever to do. This, presumably, is to say that from earliest times men have believed in, and have accepted the fact of, spirit possession. All abnormal behaviour, whether works of wisdom, feats of strength and prowess, or even antics in which no man in his senses would permit himself to indulge – all abnormal behaviour of whatever kind was ascribed to demon-possession; but one of the first developments of Jehovah-worship was to describe every manifestation of spirit-possession as definitely due to the *ruach-adonai.* Two clear instances of such transferences are Gen. xxxii. 22–32 (Jacob at Penuel), and Exod. iv. 24 (Moses at the inn), where in each case an original demon has become Jehovah. Even though the idea of witches and wizards lived on in popular superstition as vigorously as in popular English thought of yesterday, so that more than one king of Judah receives commendation for having positively and finally exterminated them all, Jehovah became established as the only source of power, and the *ruach-adonai* as the only means by which a man could receive that divine power. We may think this early view to be crude, or even erroneous. It was many years ago; we claim to be wiser than they in the ways of God to men. In any case, the fact remains that it was one of the paths which led to monotheism. For us, it may be a timely reminder that monotheism, like patriotism, is not enough. It depends what kind of monotheism it is, and what kind of patriotism.

So long as Hebrew ideas of God were non-ethical, there was naturally nothing incongruous in thus ascribing every kind of unusual behaviour to domination by the *ruach-adonai*. With the rise of the ethical prophets of the eighth century, the distinction between good and bad was perforce gradually extended to all spheres of conduct. Already in 1 Samuel the effect of this ethicizing process is seen. Saul seems always to have been subject to fits of ungoverned behaviour. All such experiences as befell him between the time of his anointing (1 Sam. x. 1) and the time of David's anointing are ascribed, whatever they are, to the *ruach-adonai*. On the contrary, in respect of such experiences as befell him after the anointing of David (1 Sam. xvi. 13), the sacred writer carefully avoids the use of the term *ruach-adonai*. The process of dissimilation has not, however, gone far enough to deny that the *ruach* by which he was then dominated was from Jehovah. 'Now the *ruach-adonai* had departed from Saul, and an evil *ruach* from the Lord troubled him' (1 Sam. xvi. 14). Here the abnormal behaviour is still regarded as being due to a *ruach* from *adonai*, though no longer to the *ruach-adonai*. In the next verse a further development is found. It was an evil *ruach-elohim*. The personal name Jehovah is not used, but in its place the general Semitic word for God which can be used of other gods than the god of Israel. And yet, though Saul is possessed by an evil *ruach-elohim*, and no longer by the *ruach-adonai*, his behaviour is still described as 'prophesying' (1 Sam. xviii. 10). Cf. 1 Sam. xix. 18–29, where the *ruach-elohim*, not evil and not the *ruach-adonai*, makes them all prophesy. Or, again, it could not be denied that the court prophets who prophesied falsely to Ahab (1 Kings xxii. 1–28) were inspired by Jehovah. Micaiah's explanation was that Jehovah had sent a lying spirit in order to entice Ahab to his doom. Here, remarkably, the *ruach* is personified, uniquely except that we may associate it with such pictures as that of the heavenly court described in Job i. 6–12. Similarly Jehovah is represented (Judges ix. 23) as having sent an evil *ruach* (i.e. a spirit to stir up trouble, not here in any way personified) between Abimelech and the men of Shechem, in order that Abimelech might the more speedily come to that timely, but unpleasant, end which the sacred writer is sure that he deserved.

The process is not complete even in Hosea. He blames both priest and prophet for the rebellious apostasy of Israel. He declaims: 'The prophet is a fool; the man that hath the spirit is mad' (ix. 7). He still defines the prophet as the man possessed by the *ruach*, but he can be a fool for all that.

The full and true prophetic inspiration appears in Mic. iii. 8: 'For truly I am full of power by the *ruach-adonai*, and of judgement, and of might, to declare unto Jacob his transgression, and to Israel his sin.' The process is complete. The *ruach-adonai* is that pre-eminent gift of power from the Lord by which a prophet is enabled, in words of grace and truth, to proclaim the ways of God to men. More than 'enabled', he is compelled. The testimony of Balaam is the witness of the prophet in every age, when the Spirit of the Lord has come upon him: 'If Balak would give me his house full of silver and gold, I cannot go beyond the word of the Lord, to do either good or bad of mine own mind: what the Lord speaketh, that will I speak' (Num. xxiv. 13). Cf. Amos iii. 8; Mic. ii. 7.

It is not permissible to find this marked and definite ethical-religious content in the description of the effect of the descent of the *ruach-adonai* on Saul, whereby he was 'turned into another man' (1 Sam. x. 6). This is the gift of that 'mana' which is a feature of primitive belief. So also for David, pre-eminently for Moses, and also for Elijah. Such men have more-than-human power. Elisha has a 'double portion' of such 'mana', and this is so powerful that even when he was dead a corpse revived immediately on coming into contact with his bones (2 Kings xiii. 21; cf. Ecclus. xlviii. 13). This is on the same lines as the many primitive elements in the Elijah-Elisha traditions. The references to Joshua are of the same type (Num. xxvii. 18; Deut. xxxiv. 9; both P). This 'mana' is the '*ruach-Stoff*' of which Volz (p. 23) writes, 'It is not anything personal (*nicht etwas Personhaftes*), but a stuff, a fluid'. Originally the preposition 'in' is used of this continued possession of 'mana', and the preposition 'upon' of sudden and particular accessions of power. The man in whom this 'mana' dwells permanently is 'a man of God'; Deut. xxxiii. 1; Joshua xiv. 6 (of Moses); elsewhere, of Samuel, of Elijah, and most of all of Elisha. Of the same type, but more advanced in theory, is the gift of *ruach-adonai* to the seventy elders. They receive 'mana' from Moses, but the gift comes to them directly from Jehovah, even though two of them remain in the camp, and are not enveloped in the cloud (Num. xi. 23–9). They all 'prophesied' when first the *ruach* rested upon them (xi. 25), but never again, though the power of the spirit (mana) remained with them to enable them to act as judges under Moses. It was by the 'mana' of these men, Moses, Joshua, and the seventy elders, that Israel was led of God from Egypt to Canaan. They were men of strange and wondrous power, terrible in wrath and mighty in deed and counsel. A late prophet describes it otherwise: 'Where is He that put His holy spirit in the midst of them?' (Isa. lxiii. 14; cf. Hag. ii. 5) – 'holy', of course, not from any suggestion of personification, nor as any forecast of the doctrine of the Third Person of the Trinity, but because it is of God, and not of man. Compare Dan. v. 14, where the Aramaic 'the spirit of the gods' is translated 'holy spirit' in the Septuagint, but 'the spirit of God' in Theodotion.

In exilic and post-exilic writings the *ruach-adonai* is the power by which the prophet is inspired (Neh. ix. 30; 2 Chron. xv. 1; &c.). The phrase was not used by Isaiah of Jerusalem (unless xi. 1–9 be from his hand), nor by Jeremiah, but both certainly know the same compelling power (Isa. vi. 8; Jer. i. 8, xx. 9, 11; and 'thus saith the Lord'). The two ideas are combined in Ezek. xi. 5: 'And the *ruach-adonai* fell upon me, and he said unto me, Speak, Thus saith the Lord.' The *ruach-adonai* also is to bring in the New Age, and, as often in passages influenced by Deutero-Isaiah, this age is to be characterized by extraordinary fertility of fold and field (Isa. xxxii. 15). Jehovah says of the Servant, 'I have put My spirit upon him' (Isa. xlii. 1). The restoration promised both by Ezekiel and by Deutero-Isaiah is to be by the power of the Spirit of God (Ezek. xxxvi. 26 f., xi. 19, xxxix. 29; Isa. xliv. 3; and, of a later time, Zech. xii. 10).

To the greatest degree Messiah is to be inspired by the *ruach-adonai*. This appears from Isa. xi. 1 and lxi. 1 f., the latter being the lesson from the Prophets which our Lord read at Nazareth (Luke iv. 18 f.), and claimed its fulfilment that very day. Compare the Zadokite fragment in Charles's *Apocrypha and Pseudepigrapha*, ii. 10, 'And through His Messiah He shall make them know His holy Spirit'. Indeed, in the glorious days of King Messiah, the power of the Spirit of God is no longer to be confined to this one or that one. One of the songs of the New Age (Joel ii. 28 f.) is that God will pour out His spirit upon all flesh, as though the fervent prayer of the Man of God, unique in Old Israel, was at last to be answered, 'Would God that all the Lord's people were prophets, that the Lord would put His spirit upon them' (Num. xi. 29); and, indeed, more than answered, for even the servants and handmaids will prophesy, and the spirit will be poured upon all flesh.

2. THE SPIRIT IS LIFE

A live man breathes; a dead man has ceased to breathe. To the Hebrew, therefore, the breath is the life, equally with the blood. Accordingly, 'the Lord God . . . breathed into his nostrils the breath [*neshamah*] of life, and man became alive' [*nephesh chayyah*; *nephesh* being that which is alive in contrast to that which is dead] (Gen. ii. 7 f.; J). The word *neshamah* means ordinary, normal breathing, in contrast to *ruach*, which in this connexion signifies violent, abnormal breathing. There is no suggestion here of a divine element in every man, a necessary divine spark in the soul. No idea could be more foreign to Hebrew thought. The statement of Hos. xi. 9, 'I am God and not man', is true of every stage of Old Testament religion. Gen. ii. 7 is an anthropomorphic ascription to God of life in man, similar to other passages in the same account – God walking in the garden, or making coats for the guilty pair.

This idea, that the breath of God is the source of life in man, is found in various exilic and post-exilic passages. *Neshamah* is paralleled with *ruach*. They are two aspects of the same divine act, the one the process, and the other the result in life and power. Cf. Job xxvii. 3, xxxiii. 4, xxxiv. 14 f.; Isa. xlii. 5; Ps. civ. 29 f. The tendency is for *ruach* to displace *neshamah*; cf. Gen. vi. 17, vii. 15 (both P), and Gen. ii. 7 (J), and doubtless this is due in part to development from the cruder anthropomorphic descriptions.

On the basis of the *ruach* of God as the source of life, representing the life-creating activity of God, we explain Gen. i. 2 (P): 'The *ruach-elohim* was brooding upon the face of the waters.' In this way the primeval chaos became capable of supporting life. Similarly also for Ps. civ. 30: 'Thou sendest forth Thy spirit, they are created; Thou renewest the face of the earth.' Here the living creatures which receive life are not men alone, but also the beasts of the field, and even the earth itself springs to new life. Ecclesiastes goes further, holding that man and beast have the same *ruach* (iii. 20 f.), but this is not the normal attitude of the Old Testament, even though it is found also in the first half of Ps. xlix., where, however, it is carefully corrected in the second, and later, half.

In Isa. xl. 13 – 'Who hath directed the Spirit of the Lord?' – *ruach* is not equivalent to *nous* (intelligence) (see *Encyc. Bibl.* 4752), as against 'essence'. The writer was a Hebrew poet, and not a Greek philosopher. He meant that creative power, native to Jehovah alone, by which, without instruction from any puppet-god of Babylon, He created all things, spanned the heavens with His hand, and spread them out like the curtains of a Bedawy's tent.

3. THE SPIRIT IS POWER

Equally with 'life', the spirit is 'power'. Indeed, it is doubtful if the idea of power is ever far removed from the word *ruach*. In Ezekiel the two phrases 'the Spirit of the Lord' and 'the hand of the Lord' are, for the most part, interchangeable. Cf. Isa. viii. 11; 2 Kings iii. 15; Jer. xv. 17; Mic. iii. 8; Judges xiv. 6, xv. 14; Isa. xi. 2; and especially Zech. iv. 6.

We have seen that *ruach* involves abnormal, violent breathing in contrast to *neshamah*, ordinary, steady breathing; further, that one of the most primitive ideas associated with *ruach* is that a man so possessed is no longer in control of his faculties. In this way, *ruach* comes to be used of powerful emotions, those dominating emotions which can hurry a man headlong to disaster. Hosea (iv. 12, v. 4) believed Israel powerless to reform. He could therefore speak of a 'spirit [*ruach*] of adulteries' because of which Israel 'could not frame their doings to return to God'. In Num. v. 14 f. (P), that determination by which a man is driven to the final, deadly test of his wife's faithfulness is a '*ruach* of jealousy'. We would say his jealousy had got the better of him;

the Hebrew said he was possessed by a *'ruach* of jealousy'. Both they and we are semi-personalizing an emotion. (It is most curious to see how some writers continuously emphasize the Hebrew way of personalizing things, feelings, and corporate bodies, as though this were a remarkable and unique trait. There is, in this habit of thought, not such a tremendous difference between them and us.) These 'spirits' can come upon men just as strongly as that *ruach-adonai* which rushes on a man (Judges xv. 14), or which a primitive age believed lifted a man up and carried him none knew where (1 Kings xviii. 12; 2 Kings ii. 16; and the remarkable parallel in the New Testament story of Philip the Evangelist. Whoever is responsible for the basic details of those first chapters of Acts knew exactly what the Old Testament meant by *ruach-adonai*). The word is used of the dominating characteristic of character and disposition: Isa. xix. 3, xxix. 10, liv. 6, lxvi. 2; Job vii. 11; Gen. xxvi. 35; Ps. li. 17; 2 Kings xix. 7 (i.e. a *ruach* of uneasiness and fear). In Proverbs, *ruach* is used in a wider sense, though still of that trait which is the key to the character, xvi. 19, 18, xiv. 29, xvi. 2 (i.e. tests character). Similarly Exod. xxxv. 21; Ps. li. 12; Num. xiv. 24. When *nephesh* and *ruach* are used in such semi-psychological senses, *nephesh* is nice and quiet and gentle, but *ruach* is strong and overpowering, like the rush and crash of the storm wind. A man can control his *nephesh*, but it is the *ruach* which controls him. And so *ruach* can be used of those profound emotions by which a man is stirred to the depths, or by which he is prostrated; Gen. xlv. 26 f.; Joshua v. 1; 1 Kings x. 5; Gen. xli. 8; 1 Kings xxi. 5; Judges xv. 19; 1 Sam. xxx. 12; Ps. cxliii. 7; Ps. li. 17. It is used of God – 'grieving His Holy Spirit' – though here (Isa. lxiii. 10) it may be merely a synonym for the Sacred Name (cf. Pss. cvi. 33 and cvii. 11). At the same time, certainly in all earlier Old Testament writings and generally throughout, where the writer finds himself involved in speaking of a man's 'spirit' or 'soul', he avoids using *ruach*, and uses *leb* (heart; Jer. iv. 19, &c.), or *nephesh* (2 Kings iv. 27; Isa. liii. 11). The reason for this appears in the next paragraph.

4. SPIRIT IS NOT FLESH

The Hebrews made a firm and clear contrast between *ruach* (spirit) and *basar* (flesh). The first was from above, the second from below. An individual was something formed out of dust into flesh, and held together by *ruach*, so that for a while it was a *nephesh*. Without this *ruach*, which came from God, belonged to Him, and would one day return to Him, man, being *basar*, was nothing but dust. *Ruach* is separate from dust, different from flesh, and in contrast is the source of life and power. The clearest example is Isa. xxxi. 3: 'The Egyptians are men, and not God; and their horses flesh, and not spirit.' This passage is fundamental to the whole doctrine of the Spirit of God in the Old Testament, and everywhere else for that matter. *Ruach* belongs to God; flesh is definitely of man in contrast to God. That is the root difference. Flesh has no power, no strength, no life, no anything but dead dust. That is why it is folly to trust in Egypt, or in anything that Egypt stands for, either then or now. There is no strength and no quietness, nor confidence (the modern word is 'security'), apart from the *ruach-adonai*. The only strength is in the *ruach-adonai*. This is brought out clearly by the Septuagint translation here, where *ruach* is translated 'help'. It is because God has always known the utter helplessness of flesh that He has mercy upon us; cf. Ps. lxxviii. 39.

This distinction between spirit and flesh is found clearly in the primitive Gen. vi. 1–8. In spite of the two well-known cruces in this passage – the meaning of the word translated 'strive' and the reading 'for that he also is' – the meaning is fairly clear. The children born of these mixed marriages are half-human and half-divine. They are therefore half-*basar* and half-*ruach*. The one means death, and the other life. The strife between death and deathlessness is summarily ended by God, who gives *ruach* the power for one hundred and twenty years, when *basar* triumphs with death, for where there is *basar* there must of necessity be death.

Whilst *ruach* is definitely not flesh, it is associated with it in that it vitalizes it. The idea of consubstantiation provides a partial analogy. This is the truth in all sacramental ideas, both in the Sacraments of the Church and in the loose way in which the phrase 'sacrament of Nature' is used. It is God who meets us there, and there is the same separation between God and the elements, and between God and Nature, as there is between *ruach* and *basar*.

And so we come to the phrase first found in Num. xvi. 22, xxvii. 16 (P), and frequent in later Jewish writings (cf. Book of Enoch), 'God of the spirits of all flesh' – that is, the God who gives to each man of flesh that *ruach* by which he lives. Here we approach the idea of a separate *ruach* in each man, for this is different from such phrases as 'a troubled spirit'. The steps are such passages as Ezek. iii. 14; Hag. i. 14; Dan. v. 20; Ezra i. 5; Prov. i. 23; Job xx. 3; and particularly Job xxxii. 8, 18, xvii. 1. Always the *ruach* of a man is from God, though in Zech. xii. 1 the idea of an individual *ruach* in each man has developed so that the prophet can say, 'And formeth the *ruach* of man within him'.

There is one passage which is incapable of translation because in it the continued use of *ruach* involves almost every shade of its meanings, both original and derived. The passage is Ezek. xxxvii. 1–14, the story of the 'wind' (*ruach*) animating the dry bones of Israel. It is impossible to say when *ruach* here means wind, spirit, life, breath, or power, and for the most part all the meanings are involved.

This passage, Ezek. xxxvii. 1–14, brings us to the main reason why the word *ruach* is used at all. If it were simply that a man has breath and therefore lives, the word would be *neshamah*, not *ruach*. It is *ruach* because here, as everywhere else in religion, it is a case of God first and man afterwards. The association of *ruach* with God is through the wind of the desert; not gentle zephyrs and soft warm breezes, but storm and tempest and overwhelming might. For this reason *ruach* always involves the idea of power, the power that makes 'the cedars of Lebanon' 'skip like a calf', that 'shaketh the wilderness of Kadesh, and strippeth the forests bare' (Ps. xxix). From the association of Jehovah with the storm-wind comes the equation of the *ruach-adonai*, the 'blast of his nostrils', and his shattering wrath. Cf. Exod. xv.; Job iv. 9; Isa. xxviii. 6, iv. 4, xl. 7. In Ezek. xxxix. 29 the

Hebrew text has *ruach*, and intends that *ruach-adonai* by which the New Age will come to be. Septuagint, however, has *thumos*, 'wrath', referring to the wrath of past judgements.

There remain three passages to which special reference must be made.

(*a*) Ps. cxxxix. 7: 'Whither shall I go from Thy spirit, or whither shall I flee from Thy presence?' Here the parallel *panim* (presence, lit. face) shows that chiefly we have here a synonym for the Sacred Name. There is no question whatever of the idea of an all-pervading Spirit of God, some sort of divineness in all created things. 'His face' emphasizes His presence, and 'His Spirit' emphasizes His power.

(*b*) Isa. xxxiv. 16: 'For my mouth, it hath commanded [better, after LXX, 'his mouth'], and His Spirit it hath gathered them.' Again, there is a parallelism, and what personification there is applies to the Divine Word equally with the Divine Spirit. Cf. 2 Sam. xxiii. 2.

(*c*) Isa. xlviii. 16: 'The Lord God hath sent me and His Spirit.' The problem here is very ancient, and turns on whether 'His Spirit' is object or subject. If it is subject, then we have the Spirit of God acting separately from, though in conjunction with, God. This distinction is found nowhere else in the Old Testament. If it is the object, then Rabbi Sa'adya was right when he translated, 'The Lord God hath sent me with His Holy Spirit', i.e. with that *ruach-adonai* which is the inspiration of the prophets.

In these passages there is undoubtedly some sort of personalization of the *ruach-adonai*, but it passes very little beyond that style of thought and speech which is necessarily common to all mankind. Indeed, it is impossible to speak of the *ruach-adonai* at all without personalizing the idea to some extent. The most the Hebrews did was to approach that half-dreamed, intangible representation which appears in Job iv. 15.

In the Old Testament, then, *ruach* is of God, and not of man. For this reason the term 'Holy Spirit' can rightly be used. This *ruach* is a condition of life, but most of all it stands for power, and the *ruach-adonai* is the power of God in and through the lives of men. This shows itself clearly in the Jewish ideas of Pentecost and in the story of Acts ii. Pentecost was the day of power. This is shown by the early Jewish readings and psalms for the day, Exod. xix.; Hab. iii.; Ezek. i.; Pss. xxix. and lxviii. All four involve a display of the overwhelming power of God. All the phenomena of His coming are found also in Acts ii., except only the earthquake, and that appears in Acts iv. 31. The descent of Holy Spirit at

Pentecost is not gentle as a dove, but tempestuous and all-powerful. (See, further, *Expository Times*, May 1932, p. 379 f.)

(b) *The Spirit of God in the Apocrypha and Pseudepigrapha*

Limitations of time and space demand that we should deal only with such writings as are found in the Apocrypha, together with the Ezra-Apocalypse and the Book of Enoch. A detailed and comprehensive study of the Spirit of God in Jewish literature generally is to be found in an article by Professor R. B. Hoyle in the *Encyclopaedia of Religion and Ethics*, vol. xi., pp. 784–803, and, for those who read German, in Volz, *Der Geist Gottes*, 1910.

Generally speaking, Old Testament usage is followed throughout, except in the Wisdom of Solomon, though necessarily the Greek words *pneuma* and *psyche* are used. The general tendency of Septuagint is followed, whereby *psyche* (soul) tends to be used psychologically, and *pneuma* (spirit) represents the stricter uses of *ruach*.

(a) *Tobit* (pre-Maccabaean, Egyptian). In iii. 6, it is the spirit of a man which ensures his living: 'Command my spirit to be taken from me that I may be released, and become earth.' We have here a development from Zech. xii. 1.

THE SPIRIT OF GOD IN JEWISH THOUGHT

(b) *Ben Sirach* (pre-Maccabaean, Palestinian). The Jewish tradition is followed, except that, after Proverbs, the creative function of the *ruach-adonai* is performed by Wisdom (i. 9, xxiv. 3). The spirit is the prophetic inspiration (xlviii. 12, xvi. 25), or ensures the continuation of life (xxxiv. 13). On the other hand, we find 'bitterness of soul' (vii. 11; cf. 2 Kings iv. 27). In the Revised Version, which is from the Greek, xvi. 17 reads, 'For what is my soul in a boundless creation?' but the original was (see Charles): 'What is my soul among the mass of the spirits of all the children of men?' Here 'my soul' is equivalent to 'I', as often in the Old Testament, and the use of 'spirits' compares with that in Tobit iii. 6.

(c) *Judith* (Maccabaean, Palestinian). In xiv. 6, fainting under the stress of deep emotion is described as the failing of spirit (cf. Gen. xlv. 26 f., &c.). With 'Let all Thy creation serve Thee, for Thou spakest and they were made; Thou didst send forth Thy spirit, and it builded them. And there is none that can resist Thy voice' (xvi. 14), compare Ps. civ. 30 and the parallelism of Word and Spirit in Isa. xxxiv. 16, together with the general ideas of the irresistible power of the Spirit of God.

(d) *2 Maccabees* (c. 50 B.C., Alexandrian). No longer do we find 'uplifted in spirit', but 'in mind' (v. 17, *dianoia*), 'in heart' (v. 21, *kardia*), or 'soul' (vii. 12, *psyche*, here meaning courage). 'Spirit' and 'life' are closely allied, both of life on this earth (vii. 22) and of a resurrection life (vii. 22, xiv. 46). A new departure is the reference to Jehovah as 'Sovereign of Spirits'. This corresponds to the phrase 'Lord of Spirits', used 104 times in the Book of Enoch, many of them earlier in date than 2 Maccabees. The phrase belongs to the time of a developing belief in angels, elemental spirits, and spirits of the air, both good and bad. The reference is probably to these incorporeal spirits, and not to the spirits of men, either during this present life or after it. In the earlier, and Palestinian, 1 Maccabees there is no reference to 'spirit', but continuously all strength and power are regarded as coming from heaven (i.e. from God).

(*e*) *Baruch* (*c*. A.D. 78, Palestinian). In ii. 17, breath is regarded as essential to life, 'the dead . . . whose breath is taken from their bodies', and the two phrases 'the soul in anguish, the troubled spirit' (iii. 1), are both in accordance with Old Testament tradition (2 Kings iv. 27; Gen. xxvi. 35; &c.).

(*f*) *Ezra Apocalypse* (*c*. A.D. 100, Palestinian). There is nothing in the Apocalypse which is not in line with Old Testament tradition, any developments being those necessitated by the belief in a resurrection, and the growing belief in elemental spirits. This is true also of the contemporary, and in some respects antagonistic, Apocalypse of Baruch. 'Spirit' is used of profound emotion (iii. 3, xii. 5; cf. 'soul' in v. 14); of being 'converted to a different spirit' (vi. 26; cf. Num. xiv. 24). There is the old association between life and breath (iii. 5, vi. 48, vii. 75). Even 'My Son the Messiah shall die, and all in whom there is human breath' (vii. 29). The word 'spirit' is used for that which has life after death (vii. 78), and in vi. 41 we find the account of the creation of the 'spirit of the firmament'. Here 'spirit' corresponds to the 'angel' in Enoch, and belongs to the class of elemental spirits.

(g) *Enoch* (pre-Christian and part probably pre-Maccabaean, Palestinian). Here, for the most part, 'spirit' is used where we would use 'soul', i.e. for that in man which survives death, and is different from the body (lxvii. 8 f.; also x. 15, xxii. 3, &c.). In lx. we find references to the spirits of the elements, and in xv. 7 f. to the 'spiritual ones of heaven' and 'evil spirits upon the earth', 'who are produced from the spirits and flesh' (cf. Gen. vi. 1–8). We have already mentioned the frequently repeated title of God, 'the Lord of Spirits'.

(h) *Wisdom of Solomon* (50 B.C.–A.D. 10, Alexandrian). Here we find a considerable change. The writer's own belief is that Wisdom alone was the Creator, and whilst, like Ben Sirach, he identifies Wisdom with the Spirit of God, his Wisdom is Greek rather than Hebrew. Indeed, he goes much further than a mere identification, for he equates the Spirit of God with the Stoic idea of a world-soul. He holds that the incorruptible Spirit of God is in all things (xii. 1), that it fills the world and holds all things together (i. 7), and that it is the source of knowledge in man of the ways of God (ix. 7). In this last he is orthodox enough, but not when he holds that the spirit which is in all things, pervades and penetrates all things by reason of her pureness, is that same power which passes into holy souls, and makes them friends of God and prophets (vii. 20–7, xi. 1).

It will be seen that, whereas in the Apocrypha generally Old Testament ideas of the *ruach-adonai* and the *ruach* of men are followed, yet in the Wisdom of Solomon we have something very different. In the Old Testament, except only for that first brooding over ('over', not 'in' or 'through') the primeval chaos, the *ruach-adonai* is essentially the power of God in and through men. In this attempt, due to Hellenistic influence, of the author of Wisdom to fit his religion into his philosophy, we have the beginning of a movement which has confused religion with philosophy. From it spring the errors of humanism, and the dangerous, we believe erroneous, identification of the work of the Holy Spirit in the hearts and lives of men with the power that makes the grass grow green.

II

THE SPIRIT IN THE NEW TESTAMENT

by

VINCENT TAYLOR, Ph.D., D.D.

II

THE SPIRIT IN THE NEW TESTAMENT

THE MOST IMMEDIATE and striking impression regarding the origin and progress of early Christianity which we gain from the New Testament is the strong consciousness of the first believers of being under the power and direction of the Spirit of God.

When the first Christians looked back to the beginnings of the Church, they recalled that Jesus had charged the Apostles not to depart from Jerusalem, 'but to wait for the promise of the Father', which they had heard from the lips of Jesus (Acts i. 4; cf. Luke xxiv. 49); and they cherished, as a word of His, the declaration: 'Ye shall receive power, when the Holy Spirit is come upon you: and ye shall be my witnesses both in Jerusalem, and in all Judaea and Samaria, and unto the uttermost part of the earth' (Acts i. 8). Probably these words reflect the subsequent experience of the Church; and, indeed, this very question is one that we shall have in mind throughout our study of the sayings of Jesus about the Spirit. There can be no doubt, however, that from the Acts, as still more certainly from the Epistles, we learn the mind and temper of primitive Christianity, and, for the moment, this is our main concern.

In the Acts it is remarkable how naturally ideas and terms associated with the Spirit are quietly assumed. The indispensable quality to be possessed by the men chosen to 'serve tables' is that they should be men 'of good report, full of the Spirit and of wisdom' (vi. 3). When Peter defends his action in respect of Cornelius, his claim is: 'The Spirit bade me go with them, making no distinction' (xi. 12), and the confirmation of his revolutionary step is the gift of the Spirit to the Gentiles: 'If then God gave unto them the like gift as he did also unto us, when we believed on the Lord Jesus Christ, who was I, that I could withstand God?' (xi. 17). The first question which Paul is represented as addressing to 'certain disciples' at Ephesus, is: 'Did ye receive the Holy Spirit when ye believed?' (xix. 2), and this representation is in striking agreement with his words to the Galatians, in which the reception of the Spirit is tacitly regarded as the equivalent of what we to-day think of as 'the acceptance of Christianity': 'This only would I learn from you, Received ye the Spirit by the works of the law, or by the hearing of faith?' (Gal. iii. 2). Baptism, in the Acts, is closely associated with the receiving of the Spirit, both as a consequence (cf. ii. 38, ix. 17 ff.) and as a pre-condition. On the Day of Pentecost Peter's hearers are summoned to repentance and baptism with the promise: 'Ye shall receive the gift of the Holy Spirit' (ii. 38), while, after his address to Cornelius, Peter cries: 'Can any man forbid the water, that these should not be baptized, which have received the Holy Spirit, as well as we?' (x. 47). And so the emphasis continues all through St. Luke's account. Paul goes on his last visit to Jerusalem 'bound in the Spirit', 'not knowing', as he says, 'the things that shall befall me there: save that the Holy Spirit testifieth unto me in every city, saying that bonds and afflictions abide me' (xx. 22 f.).

We might be inclined to ascribe this emphasis to some peculiar feature in the theology of St. Luke, were it not for the fact that it appears also in the Epistles of St. Paul. There are nearly one hundred and twenty references to the Spirit in the Pauline writings; and, indeed, in the New Testament as a whole, the only books which fail to mention the Spirit are James (but see iv. 5) and 2 and 3 John.

It is impossible, in this Lecture, to describe, or even to summarize adequately, the ideas which

St. Paul associates with the Spirit. In 1 Thessalonians, his earliest letter, he urges his new converts not to 'quench' the Spirit (v. 19), and in 2 Thessalonians he speaks of the fact that God had chosen his readers from the beginning 'in sanctification of the Spirit and belief of the truth' (ii. 13). In Galatians 'the fruit of the Spirit' is described in a catalogue of gifts and graces which is among his best-known words: 'love, joy, peace, longsuffering, kindness, goodness, faithfulness, meekness, self-control' (v. 22). Christians are to live and walk 'by the Spirit', not being 'vainglorious, provoking one another, envying one another' (v. 25 f.). In this connexion it is inevitable that we should think of the eighth chapter of the Epistle to the Romans. The language here is not merely that of sober reflection; it is that of religious ecstasy. 'Ye are not in the flesh, but in the spirit', cries the Apostle, 'if so be that the Spirit of God dwelleth in you' (viii. 9). Carried along by his exultation, he declares that 'if any man hath not the Spirit of Christ, he is none of His' (viii. 9), and, in the same breath, speaks of 'the Spirit of him that raised up Jesus from the dead' dwelling in his readers and quickening their mortal bodies (viii. 11). Led by the Spirit of God, they are 'sons of God', for they have received 'not the spirit of bondage again unto fear', but 'the spirit of adoption, whereby we cry, Abba, Father' (viii. 15). 'The

Spirit himself beareth witness with our spirit, that we are children of God: and if children, then heirs; heirs of God, and joint-heirs with Christ' (viii. 16 f.). Further, the Spirit helps our infirmity in respect of prayer; He 'maketh intercession for us with groanings which cannot be uttered' (viii. 26). His prayer for the saints in Rome is that they may be filled with joy and peace in believing, that they may abound in hope, 'in the power of the Holy Spirit' (xv. 13).

In the Corinthian correspondence there is the same deep interest in the doctrine of the Spirit. Paul recalls that his first preaching at Corinth was 'in demonstration of the Spirit and of power' (1 Cor. ii. 4). He speaks both of individuals (1 Cor. vi. 19) and of the community (1 Cor. iii. 16) as 'a temple', and of the indwelling of the Spirit. He reminds his readers that they were washed, sanctified, and justified 'in the Spirit of our God' (1 Cor. vi. 11). Amid all diversities of gifts there is 'the same Spirit' (1 Cor. xii. 4), and whether Jews or Greeks, bond or free, 'in one Spirit' they were all baptized into one body (1 Cor. xii. 13). It was not the spirit of the world which they had received, 'but the spirit which is of God', that they might know the things freely given by Him (1 Cor. ii. 12). Only 'in the Holy Spirit', he declares, do we rise to the confession that 'Jesus is Lord' (1 Cor. xii. 3).

Twice in his second letter he speaks of God's gift in 'the earnest of the Spirit' (2 Cor. i. 22, v. 5), and it is in the last verse of this letter that he pens the great benediction which has won an unrivalled place in the life of the Church: 'The grace of the Lord Jesus Christ, and the love of God, and the communion of the Holy Spirit, be with you all' (2 Cor. xiii. 14). As in all his references to the Spirit, Paul's language is that of living religious experience rather than of philosophical reflection; and for this reason one must feel suspicious of the suggestion that in 2 Cor. iii. 17 he identifies the Spirit with the living Christ. He does say: 'Now the Lord is the Spirit'; and we must reject, I think, the various ingenious attempts which have been made to represent him as saying: 'Now where the Lord is, there is the Spirit'; or, again: 'Where the Spirit is sovereign, is freedom'; but it is probable that those commentators are justified who see in this utterance a reference to the words of Exod. xxxiv. 34, which he has just quoted, and who therefore understand his meaning to be: 'Now "the Lord" in the passage I have quoted is the Spirit; and where the Spirit of the Lord is, there is liberty.'

I must resist the temptation to dwell on great Pauline passages, or even to record his teaching exhaustively, for my purpose is rather to bring home to you the dominating position which the

THE SPIRIT IN THE NEW TESTAMENT

doctrine of the Spirit has in primitive Christianity. In Philippians, Colossians, and Philemon, the references to the Spirit are fewer, but in the most cursory summary of Pauline teaching one cannot pass by the great passage in Phil. ii. 1 in which one of the grounds for the exhortation: 'Fulfil ye my joy, that ye be of the same mind, having the same love,' is the plea: 'If there is therefore . . . any fellowship of the Spirit.' Nor can we neglect the teaching of Ephesians in which the Spirit is spoken of as the believer's seal (i. 13), as the means of access (ii. 18), the source of strengthening (iii. 16), and the ground of unity (iv. 3). Most of all, the sonorous words of Eph. iv. 30 linger in the mind and tremble in the heart: 'And grieve not the Holy Spirit of God, in whom ye were sealed unto the day of redemption.'

We are not on the same height in the rest of the New Testament Epistles, but it is important to observe that the same interest in the doctrine of the Spirit persists. In 1 Tim. iii. 16, in what is perhaps a fragment of an early Christian hymn, Christ is spoken of as: 'He who was manifested in the flesh, justified in the Spirit,' but here it is doubtful whether the reference is to the Holy Spirit, or to the higher spiritual nature in contrast to 'flesh'. In 2 Tim. i. 14 the indwelling of the Holy Spirit is mentioned, and in Tit. iii. 5

reference is made to 'the washing of regeneration and renewing of the Holy Spirit'. The Epistle to the Hebrews three times introduces Old Testament quotations by a reference to the Holy Spirit (iii. 7, ix. 8, x. 15), speaks of His gifts (ii. 4), and describes apostate Christians as those who 'were made partakers of the Holy Spirit' (vi. 4). There is a doubtful reference in Jas. iv. 5, but in 1 Peter there are at least four references to the Spirit, who is associated with sanctification (i. 2), the preaching of the gospel (i. 12), the resurrection (iii. 18), and with Christians who suffer reproach for the name of Christ (iv. 14). In 2 Peter the ancient prophets are described as men who spoke from God, 'being moved by the Holy Spirit' (i. 21). Jude speaks of 'praying in the Spirit' (20), and describes men who cause secessions as 'sensual, having not the Spirit' (19). In 1 John the gift of the Spirit is the proof of the indwelling presence of Christ (iii. 24). The Spirit of God can be known by the confession that Jesus Christ is come in the flesh (iv. 2). He is identified with the truth, and, together with the water and the blood, bears witness (v. 7 f.). This is the famous passage which in the Authorized Version, without any support from the original Greek text, gives as the 'three witnesses' that bear record in heaven: 'the Father, the Word, and the Holy Ghost.'

The last writing to be mentioned is the Apocalypse. In it references to the Spirit are frequent. John speaks of himself as being 'in the Spirit on the Lord's Day', and in several passages associates his experiences as a seer with the Spirit (iv. 2, xvii. 3, xxi. 10). The Spirit also communicates with the Churches (ii. 7) and is the organ of divine revelation (xiv. 13). Together with 'the bride', He gives the Apocalyptic summons, 'Come', to those who are faithful in persecution and tribulation (xxii. 17).

This summary of the New Testament teaching outside the Gospels, although not complete, sufficiently indicates the astonishing wealth of evidence, illustrating the place which the doctrine of the Spirit occupied in the life and thought of primitive Christianity. It is not too much to say that the New Testament Church is the community of the Spirit. The Spirit enters into the most intimate relationships with believers, indwelling, teaching, revealing, sealing, guiding, inspiring, uniting, constraining, interceding, empowering. He is the life and light of God in the mind and soul of man, both in the individual and in the Church. There is scarcely an aspect of Christian belief and practice which is not in some way or other associated with His presence and power. Men's capacities are enlarged, new gifts are added, fresh aspirations are imparted, higher planes of life and conduct are made possible, as men are led, guided, and inspired by the power of the Spirit of God. It is especially notable that the fruits of the Spirit are ethical. The Early Church knew strange manifestations of the Spirit, as, for example, in that use of strange ecstatic speech which we call 'the gift of tongues'; but these are exceptional and sporadic. The broad stream of New Testament teaching concerning men 'filled with the Spirit' is related to conduct, duties, service, insight, and saintliness. The Spirit is 'Holy', and His power is directed to the sanctification and enrichment of life.

It is against this background of teaching that we must face the vital question: What place has the doctrine of the Spirit in the message of Jesus, as it is indicated in the Gospels? In this respect, we are confronted with a striking difference between the Synoptic Gospels and the Fourth Gospel, and we must seek to account for this difference. Let us take the Synoptic Gospels first.

The very limited number of sayings of Jesus with reference to the Spirit in Mark, Matthew, and Luke astonishes anyone who turns to these Gospels after reading the Epistles. Why are the sayings so few, and are those which are recorded genuine utterances of Jesus? Further, it is also remarkable that the Evangelists themselves do not introduce many references to the Spirit in narrative and editorial passages. In Mark these references are limited to the accounts of the Baptist (i. 8), the Baptism of Jesus (i. 10), and the Temptation (i. 12). Matthew adds two references to the Spirit in the stories of the Nativity (i. 18, 20) and a third in his quotation from Isa. xlii. 1–3 in xii. 18–21. Luke speaks of the Spirit several times in his Birth and Infancy stories (i. 15, 35, 41, 67, ii. 25, 26, 27). He also describes Jesus as 'full of the Holy Spirit' when He returns from the Jordan (iv. 1), of His departure 'in the power of the Spirit' into Galilee (iv. 14), and of how He rejoiced 'in the Holy Spirit' at the time of His great utterance: 'I thank thee, O Father, Lord of heaven and earth . . .' (x. 21). It cannot be said that the Synoptists resort at all freely to references of this kind in describing the mission and message of Jesus. In view of the ideas current in the period when the Gospels were written, one might reasonably expect more allusions to the work of the Spirit; and the reason for restraint in this respect can only be that the Evangelists consciously avoided comments on the story of Jesus in their fidelity to the tradition as they received it. This fact obviously bears on the question of the sayings of Jesus; it bids us pause before the suggestion, true as it is in certain

THE DOCTRINE OF THE HOLY SPIRIT

cases, that they have been modified by the theology of the Church.

It will be useful at this point to gather together the sayings which refer to the Spirit in Mark, Matthew, and Luke. Only three sayings of this kind are found in Mark: the saying on blasphemy: 'Whosoever shall blaspheme against the Holy Spirit hath never forgiveness, but is guilty of an eternal sin' (iii. 29); the introductory phrase to the quotation from Ps. cx. 1: 'David himself said in the Holy Spirit' (xii. 36); and the saying about the Spirit's guidance in the hour of persecution: 'But whatsoever shall be given you in that hour, that speak ye: for it is not ye that speak, but the Holy Spirit' (xiii. 11). Matthew records the Markan saying about blasphemy (Matt. xii. 31), but it is clear, from a comparison of Matt. xii. 32 and Luke xii. 10, that there was also a parallel version of this saying in Q, which the two later Evangelists recorded. Q also contained a version of the saying on the guidance of the Spirit in the hour of trial (Luke xii. 12 = Matt. x. 20). Matthew has the Q saying: 'If I by the Spirit of God cast out devils . . .' but Luke's version: 'If I by the finger of God . . .' is the more original form. The only other reference to the Spirit in the Matthaean sayings is the apostolic commission: 'Go ye therefore, and make disciples of all the nations, baptizing them into the name of the Father and of the Son and of the Holy Spirit' (xxviii. 19). Peculiar to Luke is the quotation by Jesus of Isa. lxi. 1 f. in the Sermon at Nazareth: 'The Spirit of the Lord is upon me' (iv. 18), and the use of the term 'Holy Spirit' in xi. 13: 'How much more shall your heavenly Father give the Holy Spirit to them that ask him?' The rendering 'good things', however, found in Matt. vii. 11, is more likely to represent the text of Q. The remaining Lukan passage which calls for notice does not mention the Spirit, but unquestionably the gift of the Spirit is meant: 'And behold, I send forth the promise of my Father upon you: but tarry ye in the city, until ye be clothed with power from on high' (xxiv. 49).

Such is the complete Synoptic record, and I think we shall agree that it is surprisingly bare. How is this to be explained? The answer, I suggest, is to be found in the principle which the form-critics are emphasizing, namely, that the preservation of both narratives and sayings in the oral period from A.D. 30 to 60 was determined by the dominating interests and problems of the primitive Christian communities. Our first thought would be that just for this reason we should expect to find many sayings about the Spirit in the Synoptic Gospels. Have we not seen already from the Epistles how greatly the Early Church was influenced, we might almost say obsessed, by the doctrine of the Spirit? But this expectation is really a misuse of the principle I have mentioned. The sayings which were preserved in Pronouncement-stories[1] were not the commonplaces of Apostolic Christianity, but those which dealt with pressing problems of belief and conduct. And if this explanation does not so easily cover collections of sayings like Q, we must remember that not a few of these sayings may be the remnants of earlier Pronouncement-stories, isolated flowers from which soil and roots have fallen away, while others of them owe their preservation to the poetic form given to them by Jesus Himself. It is not, then, so surprising as it might seem that the sayings we are considering are so few; on the contrary, their comparative rarity is entirely natural, if we consider the human conditions which determined the formation of the Gospel tradition. I believe that this is the true explanation of the fact, so clearly brought out by B. S. Easton in his study of 'The Synoptic Perspective' in his *The Gospel before the Gospels* (1928), that the beliefs current in the period to which the composition of the Gospels belong are scantily supported by sayings of Jesus. Where I should hesitate to follow him

---

[1] 'Pronouncement-stories', or 'Paradigms' (Dibelius) are short narratives which reach their climax in a saying of Jesus (e.g. Mark ii. 16 f., 18–20, 23–28, &c.).

is his assumption that later beliefs 'can be distinguished with certainty from the teachings of Jesus'. I should prefer to say 'the recorded teaching of Jesus', and to believe that much that we find in Apostolic Christianity, in connexion with the Spirit, the Church, the Eucharist, and the Cross, had its beginnings in sayings of Jesus which in the course of time passed out of recollection because they dealt with familiar and accepted things. This view is confirmed by our knowledge of the way in which memory works to-day. We easily remember the exceptional, or that which bears on a pressing practical situation, in the words of a revered teacher; the things which are familiar, however important they may be, we are prone to forget. I am well aware that in unscrupulous hands this principle might be used as an Apologetic umbrella, by which to find shelter from all kinds of sceptical storms, but that is no reason why we should leave it unused because of the fancies of contemporary fashions. My suggestion is that sayings about the Spirit are few in the recorded words of Jesus just because the doctrine was dominant.

But are the sayings genuine? Any one who is familiar with modern commentaries knows that this question is clamant. Bultmann, for example, dismisses the saying on David's Son as a 'community-product', a piece of traditional polemical

THE DOCTRINE OF THE HOLY SPIRIT

or theological material which has found its way into the recorded sayings of Jesus. He also dismisses the Markan saying on the guidance of the Spirit in the hour of trial as a 'prophecy after the event'. Similarly, Branscomb, in his recent work on Mark, in *The Moffatt New Testament Commentary*, rejects Mark iii. 28 f. – the saying on blasphemy against the Holy Spirit – as 'a product of the apostolic age'. Mark xii. 35–7, he says, 'belongs to the area of Christological debate', while Mark xiii. 11 'reveals the extent to which the community believed itself to be guided by the Holy Spirit'. Thus, every saying of Jesus in Mark, relative to the Spirit, is interred with its appropriate epitaph, and the translation which Dr. Moffatt meant to be explained is summarily explained away.

But the question of the genuineness of the sayings cannot be solved simply by criticizing critics; we must face their arguments. Even the most extreme school of criticism begins with facts; and the real problem is whether the evidence has been rightly evaluated.

There can be no doubt at all that early Christian beliefs have affected the form of some of the sayings. We have already seen that Matthew and Luke have each introduced the terms 'Holy Spirit' and 'Spirit' into sayings which originally did not contain them: Matthew in the saying:

THE SPIRIT IN THE NEW TESTAMENT

'If I by the finger of God cast out devils . . .' (cf. Luke xi. 20); Luke in the saying about the Father's readiness to 'give good things to them that ask him' (cf. Matt. vii. 11). More important still, it is probable that the great Apostolic Commission in Matt. xxviii. 19 contains early Christian terminology, when it refers to 'the name of the Father and of the Son and of the Holy Spirit', not so much because of the external evidence, and Patristic quotations in particular, but because baptism in the primitive Christian communities, as Acts viii. 16 shows, appears to have been 'into the name of the Lord Jesus'.

This, I think, is the extent to which the Synoptic sayings about the Spirit reflect later beliefs. A wholesale rejection of these sayings stultifies itself. I have already offered an explanation of the rarity of these sayings, on the assumption of the essential trustworthiness of the Synoptic tradition. What, however, is to be said, if Bultmann and Branscomb are right in finding all these sayings to be products of the Christian community? How must we explain their rarity then? On this critical theory their scarcity is an insoluble mystery, for it is impossible to say what prevented their wholesale introduction into the stream of the gospel tradition. Why, for example, does Jesus not exhort His disciples to receive the Spirit, to be filled with the Spirit, not to quench the Spirit, to manifest the fruits of the Spirit, to be 'temples' of the Spirit, to be strengthened, sanctified, sealed, united by the Spirit? This, as we have seen, is the religious vocabulary of early Christianity; and it appears in part in the Fourth Gospel. What strange fortune has excluded it from the Synoptic Gospels, where, on the hypothesis we are considering, we are handling 'products of the apostolic age', fragments of 'Christological debates', pieces of 'traditional polemical or theological material'? What strange mischance overtook the creative power of the primitive communities? Can it be that the streams of productive power dried up, like some of those rivers in Australia which flow for miles with great promise, and then are lost in the sands? Is it a case of arrested development, or was there some strange atrophy of inventiveness, some loss of nerve, if we may adapt Gilbert Murray's phrase?

In truth, we need construct none of these ingenious hypotheses; the cause is much simpler; it is nothing other than the falsity of the original assumption. It is very easy to use seductive phrases like 'products of the apostolic age', 'deposits from polemical debates', 'creations of the community', and the like, once we have learned the language; but the use of these fallacious labels does not bespeak scientific acumen or intellectual ability, but rather a certain want of humour and imagination and a limitation of judicial power. The tradition is of such a character that the best account of it we can give is the assertion of its essential genuineness.

To this general argument may be added the further consideration that at least two of the sayings – that about blasphemy against the Holy Spirit and that concerning the Spirit's guidance in the hour of peril – are attested by what are probably two lines of independent testimony, the witness of Mark and of Q respectively.

Finally, the self-evidencing character of the sayings should be considered. The saying about blasphemy against the Spirit is well attached to a credible historical situation in the life of Jesus – the attempt of the Pharisees to attribute the mighty works of Jesus to the power of Beelzebub – and illustrates that swiftness of repartee so characteristic of Jesus. The language about the inspiration of David is entirely in keeping with Rabbinical teaching. The prophecy about the Spirit's guidance is natural language on the lips of One who might well anticipate for His disciples perils which He saw crowding in upon Himself. I can see no valid reason why Jesus should not have selected Isa. lxi. 1–3 as a suitable portion of Scripture to read at Nazareth, but rather many reasons why He should have manifested the insight which such a selection reflects. And what is more natural than that at the end of His earthly life He should have spoken of the promise of the Father which should clothe His disciples with power? The only legitimate doubt is whether, as Luke places the saying, the words belong to the post-Resurrection period, for we know too little of the appearances of Jesus to be able to form any views of the conditions under which He communicated His mind to the disciples. In short, whether we consider the question of genuineness on general grounds, or from the standpoint of the sources, or in the light of the sayings themselves, the result is favourable to the tradition. The historian has every justification for refusing to find an unbridgeable gap between the teaching of Jesus and the faith of the Early Church, and the theologian may build with confidence on the tradition of His reported sayings.

It remains for us to consider the sayings of Jesus with reference to the Spirit in the Fourth Gospel.

As is well known, these sayings are more numerous than those in the Synoptic Gospels. Briefly they may be summarized as follows: In iii. 5 Jesus says: 'Except a man be born of water and the Spirit, he cannot enter into the kingdom of God,' and in iii. 6 a contrast is drawn between flesh and spirit: 'That which is born of the Spirit is spirit.' The mystery of birth by reason of the Spirit is compared in iii. 8 to the wonder of the wind. Perhaps the words about the gift of the Spirit, which is not 'by measure', in iii. 34, are meant to be those of the Baptist. In the conversation with the woman of Samaria it is declared that 'God is Spirit', but here probably there is no reference to the Holy Spirit as such (iv. 24). In the sacramental sayings in vi. the saying appears: 'It is the spirit that quickeneth; the flesh profiteth nothing: the words that I have spoken to you are spirit, and are life'; and here again a reference to the Holy Spirit is doubtful. In vii. 39 the Evangelist interprets a reference to Scripture in the words of Jesus, which no one has been able to identify, by saying: 'But this spake he of the Spirit, which they that believed on him were to receive: for the Spirit was not yet given; because Jesus was not yet glorified.' It will be seen that the only sayings of Jesus mentioned thus far which really come into consideration are those in chapter iii. which speak of Baptism and the New Birth. The remaining sayings are those of chapters xiv. to xvi. and the difficult passage in xx. 22 where Jesus commissions the disciples in the words: 'Receive ye the Holy Spirit: whose soever sins ye forgive, they are forgiven unto them; whose soever sins ye retain, they are retained.' Bultmann has reminded us that the

THE DOCTRINE OF THE HOLY SPIRIT

sayings on the Spirit in xiv.–xvi. fall into five self-contained groups, in xiv. 15–17, 25 f., xv. 26 f., xvi. 5–11, and 12–15, and he holds that these passages are insertions in the original farewell discourse. Be this as it may, their character is distinctive, and they raise difficult questions of interpretation and origin. In the first saying Jesus promises that the Father will send 'another paraclete' in answer to His own prayer, that He, the Spirit of truth, may be with them for ever (xiv. 16 f.). In the second saying the Paraclete is spoken of as the Holy Spirit. The Father will send Him in Christ's name and He will teach the disciples all things, bringing to their remembrance all that Christ said (xiv. 26). The third passage speaks of the Paraclete as sent by Christ Himself from the Father; He is described as 'the Spirit of truth, which proceedeth from the Father', and His work is to bear witness of Christ (xv. 26). In the fourth section Jesus declares that it is expedient for them that He should go away, for otherwise the Paraclete will not come. His work is to convict the world of sin, of righteousness, and of judgement (xvi. 7–11). The fifth passage declares that the Spirit's work is to guide the disciples 'into all the truth' and to 'glorify' Christ (xvi. 13 f.). As a whole, these sayings raise the problem of the Johannine sayings in its acutest form. How far are these sayings the utterances of Jesus

Himself, and in what relation do they stand to His teaching?

The course of the discussions which have now ranged for over a century have at least enabled us to reject the views which stand most widely apart. It is impossible to claim that the sayings reproduce the words of Jesus exactly as He spoke them. All too clearly the vocabulary and style are due to the Evangelist himself, and the ideas strongly suggest a Hellenistic environment, although at the same time it cannot be denied that the root conceptions are derived from the Old Testament. At the opposite extreme, it is just as impossible to maintain that the sayings are inventions, literary compositions of the Evangelist which are simply put into the lips of Jesus. The parallels with Synoptic sayings, and their fundamental Old Testament basis, strongly suggest something more than the exercise of free inventive genius. Where, then, lies the truth? Various answers are offered. The sayings, it is said, contain the thoughts of Jesus expressed in the Evangelist's language, just as the Platonic dialogues clothe the thoughts of Socrates in the language of Plato. Again, it is maintained, the sayings are interpretations of the words of Jesus; the process which lies behind them is like that embodied in the Jewish Targums, in which an Aramaic paraphrase, more or less free as the case may be, is given of the Hebrew Scriptures. I believe that each of these explanations is true so far as it goes, but I doubt if either of them goes the whole way. In many cases, no doubt, the process in the Evangelist's mind begins with an actual saying of Jesus, which has been repeatedly pondered and which ultimately finds expression in the Evangelist's idiom. But can we be certain that the process always begins with a traditional word of Jesus? Personally, I doubt if the Evangelist himself could always distinguish precisely between a saying which He had received and an idea which he believed to represent the mind of Jesus. Many of the Johannine passages 'are original sayings expressed in another idiom, but others are free productions in which the Evangelist, in the consciousness that he is led by the Spirit, expresses what he believes to be the mind of Christ'.[1]

The difficulty of this explanation is the practical one of exegesis. Can we identify sayings of either kind? I do not think that we can. This is a very disturbing conclusion, until long study of the Johannine problem, and prolonged meditation on the sayings, bring home to us the conviction that, whatever the process is, it begins with words of Jesus. Nothing less than this conclusion seems to me to do justice to the Fourth Gospel; and, if

[1] Taylor, *Jesus and His Sacrifice*, p. 220.

this is so, the question whether the sayings are the actual words of Jesus becomes of less importance. After all, we must value a book for what it is, and not for what we would like it to be. The reality, in truth, is better than our dream. That which we lose in our estimate of the Fourth Gospel is something which never existed in fact; what we gain is a view of the Gospel as it is, and as the Evangelist meant it to be – an inspired meditation upon the ultimate aspect of the teaching of Jesus. Something of this kind was doubtless in the mind of the Evangelist when he spoke of the Spirit as the Spirit of truth who should bring to mind all that Jesus had said (xiv. 26). If we say that we would prefer sayings of Jesus much nearer to His original utterances, let us remember how few are the Synoptic sayings about the Spirit. Even there we know in part and understand in part. What we are given in the Fourth Gospel is not a body of additional sayings which make good the gap left by Mark, Matthew, and Luke, but something different – inspired airs composed on the basis of original themes.

The real question, therefore, is whether the Johannine sayings express the mind of Christ; and this question, I believe, we may answer with confidence. We know little of what Jesus taught regarding baptism, but we may be sure that He traced spiritual re-birth to the power of the Spirit.

We know that He conferred a binding and loosing power upon His Church; what is more harmonious with His mind than that such authority can be rightly exercised only when men have received the Spirit? The Christian consciousness responds at once to the declaration that the Spirit is 'the Spirit of truth', that He comes from the Father, testifies of Christ, and leads men into the truth, that He convicts men of sin, of righteousness, and of judgement. How far it is true that Jesus said just these very things is an important, but insoluble, historical question; that they express the ultimate issues of His teaching cannot remain in doubt for those who believe, on the basis of the Synoptic sayings and the indirect witness of the Epistles, that He did speak of the Spirit's power and guidance as an endowment which men should receive from the Father. The Fourth Gospel is the crown of the biblical revelation concerning the Spirit because, while it begins with history and the events of time, it soars into the heavenly realms of faith and experience, revealing to us what the history and the events mean. Perhaps the best description of its nature is still that of Clement of Alexandria: 'Last of all, John, perceiving that the *bodily* facts had been set forth in the Gospels, being urged by his friends and inspired by the Spirit, composed a *spiritual* Gospel.' If this is the character of the

Fourth Gospel, however many and difficult may be the problems it creates, its witness is essential to a true understanding of the New Testament doctrine of the Spirit.

We may conclude, therefore, that, in reading the Fourth Gospel, we are studying an essential part of the evidence for the teaching of Jesus regarding the Spirit. The influence of the Christian community is to be found with far greater justice here than in the case of the Synoptic sayings, but the truest explanation of the data is that the Johannine sayings give the teaching of Jesus as elucidated and expressed by a singularly discerning mind.

While it does not fall within the scope of this Lecture to discuss the implications of New Testament teaching, it would be unpardonable to conclude this survey without a reference to the points which call for further discussion. Of the remarkable emphasis given to the doctrine in the New Testament enough has been said. Everywhere it is assumed that the Spirit is the power of the Living God in the individual, the Church, and the world. This power is not simply that of a pervading influence; it is personal, divine power working directly for ethical and religious ends. Especially does this power find expression in connexion with the revelation made in Jesus Christ; so much so that it is natural to speak of the Spirit, the Holy Spirit, the Spirit of Christ, and the Spirit of God, without any intention of making exclusive distinctions. Here is the groundwork upon which Christian theology must build. But the most significant element has not yet been mentioned, namely, the fact that Jesus Himself thought and spoke of the Spirit as the Divine Power in active manifestation. What this means depends upon what we believe concerning Jesus Christ. If we believe that He is the Son of God, as the Gospels and the Epistles represent Him to be, and as faith and experience interpret Him, the stage is set for that long process of Christian inquiry and debate which finds its least inadequate expression in the historic doctrine of the Trinity.

III

THE HOLY SPIRIT IN THE CHURCH

by

HOWARD WATKIN-JONES, M.A., D.D.

III

THE HOLY SPIRIT IN THE CHURCH

THE DISTINCTIONS DRAWN in the New Testament, especially in the writings of St. Paul and St. John, between the Holy Spirit and the Father and the Son, together with divine actions ascribed to Him, must have rested ultimately on the teaching of our Lord Himself. So the Church came to believe; and Christian theology has developed a Doctrine of the Spirit in consequence, now metaphysical, now experimental, throughout the varying periods of ecclesiastical history. It will be our task to trace the outline of different aspects of this development.

Since Theophilus of Antioch first used the word 'Triad' with reference to the Holy Trinity, there never has been, from that second century to the twentieth, any suggestion that the Christian doctrine of God is based on reason: this is a mystery which reason cannot explain, yet it is one which may to some extent be intellectually conceived. We have to wait a hundred years, however, to find the first truly systematic theologian of the Trinity in Unity, the lawyer Tertullian. It seems as if his theology was guided by the legal usage of the terms 'substance' and 'person' as meaning property and an individual who rightly held it (J. W. C. Wand, *A History of the Early Church*, p. 81); at least, in arguing with Praxeas and the Monarchians, he speaks of the Divine Unity as self-developing into threefoldness, the same whole Divine Object existing in each of the Three. Origen, at that time at the head of the Christian academy in Alexandria, ventured the opinion that the Holy Spirit derived His being from the Son; and, while he cannot be proved heterodox, he was constantly in two minds how precisely to place the Spirit in relation to the Godhead.

That learned bishop of a later age, Eusebius of Caesarea, said that the Holy Spirit 'is one of the beings that derive through the Son', which was orthodox enough; yet his Greek might just as grammatically be translated 'one of the things that were made by the Son', which would have been a very different matter. Accordingly Eusebius has often been misunderstood by theologians since; and yet he seems to have been misunderstood by theologians then – in times when it was just as possible to construe Greek incorrectly! But the Arians could make little capital out of either Origen or Eusebius. They would have nothing to do with the Sabellian confusion of the Holy Spirit with the Father and the Son; indeed, they never denied a distinct existence to the Holy Spirit. Yet their so-called Trinity was a trio of Persons who differed greatly in being and in glory, and by the year 359 even some of the Semi-Arians were openly declaring their belief that the Holy Spirit was a creature.

The Creed of the Holy Communion shows how decisively this was rejected by the Church before the fourth century ended. The great fourth-century theologians, Athanasius in part and especially the three Cappadocians, Gregory, the unhappy Patriarch of Constantinople, and the two brothers Basil and Gregory of Nyssa, insisted that the Spirit is an eternal relation *within* the Godhead. He was God Himself, and as such He was invoked upon the Bread and Wine whenever the Supper of the Lord was celebrated. And in the West any doubt there remaining was settled by Augustine, whose arguments for the place of the Holy Spirit in the one Godhead were very similar, only that he made much freer use of human analogies. This position was at once taken up by the Medieval Church.

The implications of the Trinity were thought out still more minutely by the Schoolmen: absolute equality in regard to the Divine Persons means that any two are not together greater than a third; the whole Godhead resides in each, all act in the acts of each. To this Aquinas adds much else appertaining to the divine kind of work the Spirit does – a consideration which especially appealed to the Reformers. Naturally the Deists and the Socinians revolted against the trend of all this, and the Arminians – 'a crew of Socinianized Arminians' John Owen called them – argued that the Divine Unity was guaranteed simply because the Son and the Spirit are *less* than the Father! The battle between the Church and the Unitarians of the seventeenth and eighteenth centuries in England was a conflict of wits (in large measure) on the basis of scriptural texts, and in this connexion John Wallis, a Unitarian leader, avowed that references in Scripture to a Trinity were not impressive in that he found more warrant therein for the dogma of transubstantiation! In 1690 Dean Sherlock of St. Paul's, assured that he had a simple explanation of the Trinity to offer, published a book in which he declared that the Divine Persons were three infinite Minds or centres of self-consciousness joined in one by a mutual consciousness; he in turn was accused of tritheism, while the Unitarians professed amusement and prepared for another attack.

Incidentally we may notice a contribution to the discussion interjected by Swedenborg from an angle of his own. He had, he said, often conversed with angels on the subject of the Being of God, and they had told him that Trinitarians could not possibly be admitted into heaven because they divided the Divine Being into Three. Those angels might have made themselves better acquainted with Christian theology! But all through the English debate one assertion was constantly pressed, namely, that the divine operations of the Holy Spirit reflect on His Essence and His place within the one Divine Life. 'I do not see', observes Wesley, 'how it is possible for any to have vital religion who denies that these Three are One.' This he said of what is called the Redemptional Trinity. As to theories meant to explain a metaphysical Triunity in God, he doubted their wisdom: 'It was in an evil hour that these explainers began their fruitless work. I insist upon no explication at all; no, not even the best I ever saw . . . I would insist only on the direct words, unexplained, just as they lie in the text' [1 John v. 7 (A.V.)] (Sermon 60, 'On the Trinity').

When it was asserted that the Holy Spirit 'proceeds' from the Father, it was felt that the Church had a term which was scriptural and which also differentiated this function from the 'generation' of the Son. In the course of the fourth century the East, led by the Alexandrian and Cappadocian schools, sanctioned the statement that the Spirit proceeds 'through the Son'; this was really an inference from Origen's doctrine of the eternal generation of the Son, and it served in the West until Augustine. Such an approximation to a twofold procession was regarded as stressing the Divine Unity; and, in regard to this, Dr. G. L. Prestige has pointed out the significance of the fact .that the school of Antioch, 'which declined to accept the unifying conception of the double procession, was also the school which failed to arrive at a satisfactory statement of unity in relation to the Person of Christ' (*God in Patristic Thought*, p. 255). This is a reference to the Nestorian heresy which joined the eternal Son to the man Jesus by a moral bond; it had affinities with Arianism. It could be only through a fully Divine Son that a fully Divine Spirit could proceed: such has always been the position of the Greek Orthodox Church.

Augustine, however, boldly taught the West a double procession outright – that the Spirit proceeds from the Father *and* the Son eternally, as from one Source; then, whereas he had added that He proceeds principally from the Father, the Medieval Church soon held that He proceeds equally from both. The Western belief in this double procession, which was first slipped into the Creed by an excited Council at Toledo in

589, caused much embarrassment to the Papacy until the final split of East from West in the eleventh century removed the last obstacle to its official adoption. Aquinas, in consequence, can make use of it in the course of his insistence on the unity of the Triune God. As the Holy Spirit proceeds, He unites the Trinity as the bond of the eternity of the Father and the equality of the Son as the mutual love of Them both, or as Their common life; so that no one Person can be conceived apart from the others. The Unity *is* the Trinity, and the Trinity the Unity; such was the teaching of Reformer as well as Schoolman, even though such as Calvin spoke more freely of the united working of the Trinity in the human experience of salvation. Indeed, the emphasis on the Spirit's procession from both Father and Son suited the practical outlook of the West: it was evangelical in its ring, Jesus was still present with men, working through His Spirit for their salvation. Let Arminians disagree; the Western Church stood by its view; for it was, and is, convinced that the Holy Spirit is '*distinctively* that Spirit as it comes to us from the whole life and teaching, work and personality, of Jesus Christ for our salvation' (W. L. Walker, *The Spirit and the Incarnation*, p. 90).

Something must be said at this point concerning the difficult matter of the Divine Personality of the Holy Spirit. There was little or nothing written specifically about this during the first century A.D., 'perhaps', as Professor Swete suggests, 'chiefly because the Spirit had come to glorify Jesus and not to direct attention to His own relation to God' (*The Holy Spirit in the New Testament*, p. 294). Miss Evelyn Underhill's remark that 'we most easily recognize Spirit when it is perceived transfiguring human character' goes far to explain our attitude of problem regarding any definition of 'personality' attaching to the Holy Spirit in comparison with our natural acceptance of the term as applied to Christ. Hence it may not be surprising to note that there appeared some confusion of the Spirit with the Son at the commencement of the second century. To Hermas the Spirit was God's Son; and, though the general verdict is that Hermas was no theologian, he was not alone in his uncertainty, for certain of the early Apologists equally confused the Spirit with the Logos. Next, Sabellius regarded the Holy Spirit as the third successive way in which the one Person of the Deity might be conceived; on the other hand, as will be remembered, the Arians felt sure that the Spirit was no mere impersonal energy even while they placed Him outside the Being of God. The Catholic or Great Church, however, had come by the fourth century to take the definite stand that the

Spirit should be believed to be a Divine Personality, not in any way separate from God, but rather, to use Swete's phrase, 'the indivisible Godhead subsisting and operating in one of the essential relations of His tripersonal life' (*The Holy Spirit in the Ancient Church*, p. 376).

Considerable pains have been taken to show what exactly the theologians of the Early Church meant by the word 'Person' in its Greek and Latin equivalents. Originally 'an actor's mask', it came to mean a part taken by an actor, or by any one, and therefore 'a person looked at from some distinctive point of view'. More still, adds Dr. Wheeler Robinson, was this so when the word 'hypostasis' was used, 'for this is an abstraction' (*The Christian Experience of the Holy Spirit*, p. 254). The conclusion is that early usage of these terms proves that no belief at all existed that there are three distinct centres of personality in God; to this extent it is a helpful conclusion. At the same time, the careful examination of such terms by Dr. G. L. Prestige, in his recent book, *God in Patristic Thought*, safeguards as well as clarifies what was in the mind of the Early Church. In point of fact, he says, ' "hypostasis" lays the stress on concrete independence'; it signifies that the Divine Persons are 'substantive objects'. In other words, it refers to 'God as manifest' – as an object, as compared with *ousia*, which refers to

THE DOCTRINE OF THE HOLY SPIRIT

'God as being' – as a subject. Actually the meaning of 'mask' could well be regarded as a gift to the Sabellians, in that they were ready enough to construe God as one and the same Actor assuming three masks one after the other, the Trinity being just successive manifestations of God. The mature thought of the Early Church, as Dr. Prestige reports it, was that in God there are 'three *complete* presentations of the whole and identical object'. 'God, regarded from the point of view of internal analysis, is one object; but, regarded from the point of view of external presentation, He is three objects', these three objects of presentation being identically one. 'The three presentations possess a concrete and independent objectivity.' And yet 'the sum "God+God+God" adds up, not to "three Gods", but simply to "God", because the word God, as applied to each Person distinctly, expresses a Totum and Absolute which is incapable of increment either in quantity or in quality' (pp. 113, 168 f., 177 f.). *Ousia*, or Essence, therefore, is that which is wholly in each Person; the individuality is only the manner in which the identical substance is objectively presented in each several Person. 'One and the same Divine Being is presented in distinctive objective and permanent expressions', which, so Prestige suggests, may be put thus in more modern parlance: 'In God there are three divine organs of God-consciousness, but one centre of divine self-consciousness' (p. 301). This one centre, this utter Unity, was a chief concern on the part of early Christian teachers. Gregory of Nazianzus, in the course of his fifth Oration to the Arians in Constantinople, observed that worship of any one Divine Person carries with it the worship of all Three. That is an obvious thought. But it is of interest to notice that, from the fourth century to the seventh, the idea grew that the three Persons 'contained' one another, literally 'went round about' one another, until by the seventh century a term had become concrete for its expression – 'perichoresis' or 'circumincessio', a co-inherence, the Persons receiving and permeating one another with perfect equality in the one Godhead. Thus the Holy Spirit was *in* the Father and the Son, Himself the personal completion of Their Unity. By his doctrine of the double procession, as also by his dwelling on the unity of differing activities within the human mind, Augustine passed on to the Western medieval age the pith of what has just been mentioned. The Medieval Church was attracted to the idea of the mutual love of the two Persons demanding a third Person for its perfect expression, even though it talked but figuratively; but it insisted that the whole subject could not be treated as if three individuals were

THE DOCTRINE OF THE HOLY SPIRIT

being discussed. The eternal and essential relations of paternity, filiation, and procession *are* the Father, Son, and Holy Spirit respectively; there cannot be 'otherness' in the Godhead. In Nicholas of Cusa's words, 'the Persons are not Persons save in a state of union'.

Yet the Schoolmen were but attempting to put into reasonable language what they felt were primarily truths of revelation; as touching the Holy Spirit, they held that His saving operations in the soul always indicate most surely the fullness of His personal life, though we must admit that some emphasized this more than others. Such personal allusions on the basis of Scripture, as relating to the Spirit's work, were taken up by English preachers of the seventeenth century – by Andrewes when preaching before the Court of James I, by Donne in St. Paul's, by Sterry before the Commonwealth Parliament. These men were constantly emphasizing the Divine Personality of the Spirit on the strength of the New Testament references to His work, yet all within the one life of God. John Owen states that 'a Divine Person is nothing but the Divine Essence upon the account of an especial property, subsisting in an especial manner'. Isaac Barrow, a seventeenth-century contemporary, speaks of 'a mutual inexistence of One in All and All in One', which is a reminder of the co-inherence idea a thousand years before. The whole witness of the Church is to a Personal Divine activity within the one life of God, borne out, we must add, in the deep experimental theology of the Wesleys, and set forth in modern theological works which the scope of this present Lecture does not include.

Turning now to the manifold working of the Spirit of God, we read the testimony of the Early Church to His going forth in the creation and the sustaining of the universe, at first some feeling that the Logos and the Spirit co-operate in this, then (particularly in the fourth century) this same fundamental truth becoming expanded into the belief that the powers of creation flowed from the Father, yet it was the work of the Son *through* the Holy Spirit, whose immanence sustains the created order. The Middle Ages, anxious about the Divine Unity, stressed the work of the Three Persons in the universe: Nicholas of Cusa added the quaint thought that the nature of the Triune God has accounted for the three principal classes of creatures – the spiritual, as embracing the angels; the corporeal, as embracing vegetables, animals, and the elements; and that which is both spiritual and corporeal, as embracing man. Yet, on the basis of the Divine Unity, it was felt that it is especially the Holy Spirit through whom the whole work of God becomes effective, both in regard to humanity and the universe at large.

Arminius passed on the same idea to the Modern Church. Cudworth, the Cambridge Platonist, expressed the opinion that, at creation, the Spirit of God possibly worked upon some sort of incorporeal substance or 'plastic nature', akin to the world-soul of Platonism, and has since governed Nature through that life-principle. At the same time, Cudworth insists that the Holy Spirit gave moral freedom to man, gave him soul, mind, sense, and reason, which could never arise from matter alone.

We find in this connexion that Leibnitz, though he upheld a Trinity, robbed It of all redemptional character by the determinism for which he found room in the divine scheme. But the ascription of universal activities continued to be made to the Holy Spirit expressly, Wesley, for instance, remarking that He 'governs all, not only to the bounds of creation, but through the utmost extent of space'. It must be admitted that the general position that, as Jeans has put it, 'the universe begins to look more like a great thought than like a great machine', does not specifically provide for the working of the Holy Spirit in our distinctive sense: that must continue to rest ultimately on a ground of revelation. And yet, in all the present-day discussion of God active in His universe, as well as upon it, the conception of God as immanent affords an association of ideas relative to Spirit – His Holy Spirit – which comes naturally to those who give weight to Christian opinion as developed through the centuries.

The Incarnation of our Lord was, of course, a creational activity of a unique order. Here, again, Logos and Spirit were identified at one time in the conception and birth of Jesus, though this was clarified by the fourth century. The Medieval Church pointed out that the work of the Spirit in the Incarnation did not mean that there were two Fathers in the Trinity, but that, through the Spirit, the one Father exerted His own function of Fatherhood. Schoolmen and Reformers joined in saying that the sinlessness (absence of original sin) of Christ was due to the fact of this particular work of the Spirit, and the Roman Catholic Church was developing her doctrine of the Immaculate Conception of the Virgin Mary, who was thereby declared free from original sin even as her Son. Not all the later writers in England agreed on this matter with the Reformers. The feeling was expressed that, while Christ had no original tendencies to sin, He *could* have sinned nevertheless; and if His temptations were greater than ours so also were His powers of resistance. So the Son alone was incarnate, or, as the Medieval writers put it, the whole Deity became incarnate, but in the Person of the Son alone.

Hooker agreed: 'Incarnation may neither be granted to any Person but only one, nor yet denied to that Nature which is common unto all Three' (*Ecclesiastical Polity*, v. 51. 2). Naturally the Unitarians disagreed. Priestley asserted that Christ's parents were Joseph and Mary, that His divinity was a later invention of Christian philosophers, and that it was incredible that any incarnate God should actually inhabit our small world 'in preference to any other in the whole extent of perhaps a boundless creation'. We may add that most decidedly we should not have believed it if we had not been told.

The very word 'inspiration' suggests Spirit, and it was linked with the Holy Spirit from the early days of the Primitive Church. Certain writings were gradually collected as especially inspired, and, under pressure at first from the Gnostics, an embryo New Testament was circulating before the close of the second century, and the canon of inspired scriptures was pronounced complete by Athanasius in A.D. 367. For some time in the second century the Church was troubled by such as Marcion, who could see very little difference between the God of the Old Testament and the Devil; it was a crisis indeed, for if the inspiration of the Old Testament had not been fully accepted the spiritual continuity of the Christian Church with the Church of the

THE HOLY SPIRIT IN THE CHURCH

Old Covenant would have gone, and Christianity would have been in danger of being numbered among the philosophies. But, founded on an historical rock, Christianity might be safely regarded as having been prepared for by philosophy; so philosophy had been spiritually useful, said Clement of Alexandria, though Tertullian saw nothing that was good in it. Yet it was healthy that a wide view of the Spirit's inspiration found supporters; quite likely such mental hospitality did something to assist the belief that the Spirit, in speaking through so many different kinds of persons, did not despise their natural human faculties.

There were some, like the Montanists, who believed that inspiration works through passive ecstasy, but they were in the minority in the early centuries, and this emphasis on the human element in inspired writers was continued till the Reformation. Thus the belief in 'verbal' inspiration never attracted much attention till the seventeenth century, since when it has made up for lost time! Even so, divergences of opinion arose at the Reformation on many matters. To the Reformers the written Word was the principal instrument of the Spirit, who would interpret its truth to the individual mind; whereas to the Roman Catholics both the Bible and the tradition of the Church were equally inspired, and the former must be interpreted by the inspired, and therefore infallible, authorities of the Church. This insistence on the Spirit's guidance through tradition was also characteristic of the East. English Protestantism made it clear that it was necessary that the Inspirer of the Word should also inspire its readers; and, though one of its great representatives, John Owen, could not believe that the Spirit actually dictated the words of the Bible, he did think that He suggested to its writers words which they themselves had been in the habit of using.

The Quaker doctrine of an 'inner light' is well known. It was an illuminating power of the Spirit directly operating on the mind – the mind of *any* man. Scripture was of course inspired, and the mind illumined by the Spirit cannot but be a living witness to the truth which Scripture contains. Yet the Quaker doctrine did come as a relief to the theory of verbal inspiration which was held by so many Puritans. Not even Scripture had to be its never-failing test, much less natural reason. The general testimony, however, was that the Bible was inspired by the Holy Spirit in a special manner to which the spiritual consciousness could bear witness; indeed, Wesley regarded as the fundamental doctrine of the Methodists that 'the Bible is the whole and sole rule of Christian faith and practice'.

THE HOLY SPIRIT IN THE CHURCH

Throughout these later years the battle has swayed between different ideas of inspiration. The truth of progressive revelation has been far more widely appreciated, the way in which inspiration works has had much light thrown on it by the study of psychology, while accounts of how the influence of the Spirit has been seen in semi-civilized peoples through their reading of the Scriptures are modern confirmations of what the Church has continually taught. Coleridge's familiar assertion carries its own conviction: 'Whatever finds me bears witness for itself that it has proceeded from a Holy Spirit.'

The mission of the Spirit of God to the world for its salvation broadened the whole vista. Since Pentecost the Spirit had been poured out in fullness: from the second century this received constant emphasis, by Arians too. There were early variations; Cyprian said that He had been poured out on the Church, Origen on the saints; but as time progressed it was allowed that He comes upon all men, though in a special manner on the Church, seeing that the sanctifying office is His pre-eminently. Thus, the later in the Early Church the wider the Holy Spirit's mission was held to be. It was a 'great extension' of the work of God as done in the Old Dispensation; it was the old gift, but in a new abundance (Swete, *The Holy Spirit in the Ancient Church*, p. 394). When the Medieval Church took up the strain, it made its characteristic comment that the mission of the Spirit conveys the entire Trinity. Further, the scope of this mission knows no limit. The Spirit is present with rational creatures of all kinds, good and evil, strengthening the good forces in the world, yet only entering the heart in response to faith. Of this outpouring the Church is the principal channel, through which the Divine Spirit comes as a fertilizing river. 'If the Holy Ghost come not, Christ's coming can do us no good,' said Bishop Andrewes, while Matthew Henry observed that, though the Holy Spirit had always dwelt in the Old Testament saints, His visible manifestation to the whole world did not take effect till Pentecost, when He came more powerfully than ever before. Here, then, was a mighty Gift actually given to the human race, to the Church, and to the souls of all who desired Him; a Gift never withdrawn.

The relation of the Holy Spirit to the Church and the sacraments has often been an occasion of controversy: it is at any rate good to know that these are questions which are being faced in a more Christian spirit and by vastly more branches of the Universal Church than ever before. To begin with, the New Testament tells us that Christ's gift of His Spirit was made, not only to the Apostles in the stricter sense, but also to the whole Church, with its priesthood of all believers. It is common knowledge how differences arose in the course of history as to what this inspired community was. The Roman Catholic belief was that the Church is a visible organism, governed unerringly by the Holy Spirit; to the Reformers generally the Church consists of all those who know God in Christ through the Word and the sacraments, and in whose hearts the Spirit dwells.

Ordination to the special ministries of the Church from early times was related to the gifts of the Spirit as then bestowed, until in the Middle Ages it was held that the power of the Spirit was thereby received for the particular functions of the priesthood, especially that of offering the Sacrifice in Church. The Reformers generally regarded ordination as the laying-on of hands by those who *recognize* the Spirit's call to the ordinand by the presence in him of the divine gifts. The Quakers, who did not deem a separated ministry a necessity, regarded the Church as a company of people assembled under the influence of the Holy Spirit and united in their belief in the fundamentals of the faith; it was a definition so broad as not rigidly to exclude even non-Christians in so far as they follow the inner light of the Spirit.

Methodism believes in itself as a branch of the Catholic Church of Christ on earth, adhering to the 'fundamental principles of the historic

THE DOCTRINE OF THE HOLY SPIRIT

creeds and of the Protestant Reformation', and proclaiming a distinctive message of experimental theology. To this end it was raised up by the Spirit of God. The Oxford Movement revived spiritual religion as well as what may be termed the 'Catholic' conception of the Church and the sacraments. On all such expressions of corporate Christian life has the blessing of the Holy Spirit rested. And may we not add with equal conviction that on all the varied ministries of the Universal Christian Community the blessing of the Holy Spirit has also rested? Dr. Streeter has shown with perfect plainness that no one form of Church Order is primitive, and that therefore no exponents of one order can, either with justice or charity, suspect the validity of those of another. Canon Raven's declaration that historic continuity is not a question of physical contact, but of identity of function and purpose (*The Church's Task in the World*, p. 110), reaches down to the spiritual foundations, and these are the things which supremely need perfect honesty and perfect love to examine. The Church of Christ is certainly a continuity, but it is a continuity of *life* – the life of the Divine Spirit – which has been the source of diversity of forms as of gifts.

Regarding the sacraments, here again the point of common emphasis was that they are channels of the Spirit's grace, media of His working. As

Swete has said, 'the third and fourth centuries tended to make the sacraments the only channel of the Spirit', and this developed into the medieval doctrine that the sacraments confer grace by virtue of their own action – *ex opere operato* – little being asserted about the operation of the Holy Spirit or about the need for faith in this connexion. The presence of the Spirit in the sacraments was stressed by the Reformers, who nevertheless insisted that no benefit could be derived from these apart from faith. Similarly the Wesleyan Methodist Conference (in 1908) declared that 'the presence of Christ by His Spirit in the sacraments is realized by the faith of His people'. Faith, however, was recognized by the Early Church as needful in Baptism, however much the ceremonies in conjunction with it became elaborated. Cleansing, sanctifying, empowering; such were the principal operations of the Spirit as taught in the early centuries. So did the Medieval Church teach that the Spirit is the source of forgiveness and grace in this sacrament, then later the Romanist Council of Trent in the sixteenth century asserted that baptism remits the guilt of original sin.

According to this, baptism is essential to salvation. Both Luther and Calvin believed that in baptism the grace of the Holy Spirit is given in response to faith; in the case of infants the faith of those who bring them is accepted on their behalf. Calvin is rather more explicit that it is the Holy Spirit who is the sole worker in the sacrament; He may indeed give His grace later on in the life of the baptized child, in the sense that baptismal grace is in no sense bound up with the elements used at the time. Luther, attracted by baptismal regeneration, held that this sacrament is necessary to salvation; Calvin held the opposite, for baptism could do no good to persons not elected to glory. Naturally, then, it could not be vital to the salvation of those who are elected: yet he did believe that it is the outward sign of our inward renewal by the Spirit. Zwingli, who may be thought of as the left-wing leader in the Reformed camp, believed that baptism is simply the outward sign of the witness of the Christian and of his entrance into God's family on earth. All the Reformers rejected the *ex opere operato* idea completely; yet their own variations, joined with considerations of the Romanist position, meant that a legacy of debate has come from their age to the Church in this, with its oscillations between baptismal regeneration on the one hand and differing degrees of Church connexion on the other.

We feel that the Methodist Church in relation to this takes something of a middle position. Thus in the Memorandum on Infant Baptism,

1936, it is stated: 'The sacrament of baptism is the "outward and visible sign of an inward and spiritual grace", and when administered to adults and received in faith, the outward sign is in itself a conscious means of grace.... In this sacrament, when administered to infants, the outward sign and the inward grace are in some ways to be distinguished. The outward act anticipates the day when the child will consciously accept the inward grace.... By adult baptism, Christians are outwardly identified with the "congregation of Christ's flock", the visible fellowship of His disciples in which the Holy Spirit dwells. This sacrament is thus, not only an outward symbol, but also a channel of inward grace.'

Regarding the Lord's Supper, there can be seen a growing sense of the working of the Holy Spirit in this ordinance, perhaps mainly as the divine vehicle of Christ's presence. The use of the invocation of the Spirit on the elements, by which some kind of change was held to take place, was common by the fourth century; and when, by the eleventh century, the dogma of transubstantiation had generally been accepted, the belief still stood, side by side with philosophical explanations of the dogma, that this change in the elements was the work of the Holy Spirit. But there was no obvious mention on the part of the Schoolmen of the Spirit's work in the hearts of the communicants;

transubstantiation was dangerously materialistic, and Luther's consubstantiation seemed little better. At least there is the assertion by Professor Heiler of Marburg that 'the normal Lutheran Communion Service is nothing but a reformed Roman Mass' (in *Northern Catholicism*, p. 480), and early in Elizabeth's reign Archbishop Grindal likened Lutherans to semi-Papists – though we may make some allowance for his strong Puritan sympathies. But the Reformers in general upheld a close connexion between the Holy Spirit and the Lord's Supper: as we partake by faith it is made by the Spirit to be a seal to us of the redeeming love of Christ; and even Zwingli, who stressed the memorial nature of the rite, allowed that the grace of Christ may be received by faith through the Holy Spirit. Calvin expressed the belief that at the Supper the Holy Spirit is present as the medium of Divine Grace; by Him the communicant is incorporated with Christ and made a sharer in His glorified body. The elements are symbols of Christ's Person in the taking of which we receive Him and the merits of His Passion and death; and all happens, as the Calvinist Synod of Dort said in 1619, 'through the Spirit by faith'. These two factors, the Spirit and faith, were especially emphasized by Wesley, who employed this sacrament as both a converting and a sanctifying ordinance.

THE HOLY SPIRIT IN THE CHURCH

The saving and sanctifying power of the Spirit is one of the great themes of the New Testament; the Pauline and Johannine writings are full of it. The life of the Early Church was also full of it. Not only what the Christians said, but also what they were, provided an increasing challenge to the Gentile world; and it is not surprising that, by the fourth century, leaders such as Augustine and the Gregorys and Basil were emphasizing in their books the Spirit's sanctifying work. Not every one agreed with what the Church proclaimed; Pelagius, for instance, cried up a sort of humanism which was examined and found terribly wanting, especially by the West. Doubtless he was right in a measure: it is possible to feed one's soul on reiterations of its filth and impotence so that the sinews of all healthy effort are cut, sometimes for ever. But to deny prevenient grace and belittle grace of any other sort – in effect, to preach a gospel of trial and yet more trial – was to pluck up the true Gospel by the roots. Whether baptism marks the beginning of the Christian life or not – Early Christians generally thought it did – it was a delusion and a snare to believe that the spiritual powers of God were not vitally needful, and still more so to go about trying to induce other people to believe it. So Christian thought swept on past such beguilings, until in the Middle Ages in the West, as also in the later East, the renewing graces of the Spirit of God were unceasingly stressed as those of the whole Deity operating through the Spirit.

The Schoolmen and the Mystics believed that justification includes sanctification, and this belief found crystallization at the Council of Trent, which declared justification to be an infusion of righteousness bestowed by the Holy Spirit through the sacraments. Granted there arose at times considerations of formalism or of human merit by which the Spirit's working tended to become obscured; yet this teaching of the Medieval Church did urge a holiness of life, a real making righteous, which looked to the Spirit of God as its source. The Reformers made a distinction between forgiving and cleansing, justifying and sanctifying, but they stated that both were actions of the Spirit, by whom alone man is remade, by faith. At the Reformation the subject revived as to the relation of the Spirit to the human will in these matters. The Romanists said that it could co-operate under the prevenient influence of the Holy Spirit, which in essence was Melancthon's position; Luther and Calvin stressed the utter impotence of the will, and disliked altogether the idea of co-operation. English Calvinism took the same course. Quakerism was much more cheerful, with its doctrine of the Spirit's inner light which not even the Fall could have quenched;

THE HOLY SPIRIT IN THE CHURCH

and Wesley, excluding the Spirit at no stage, declared that 'all true faith, and the whole work of salvation, every good thought, word, and work, is altogether by the operation of the Spirit of God' (*A Farther Appeal*, I. i. 6). The Quakers included works in justification, obliterating any distinction between it and sanctification. On the other hand, Wesley made the usual Protestant distinction very clear, thus: 'By justification we are saved from the guilt of sin, and restored to the favour of God; by sanctification we are saved from the power and root of sin, and restored to the image of God.'

On the subject of growth in the holy life there was significantly little fundamental divergence. Once again, the Spirit and faith are the basal couplet. Different minds speak in different ways, but about the one thing. 'The dove lights on no carrion,' says Andrewes. The appeal to discipleship through the attraction of Christ's *beauty* hardly sounds like a Puritan appeal, but it was, not once nor twice. 'Some think that the love of the Father and blood of the Son will do, without the holiness of the Spirit of God,' says Bunyan; 'but they are deceived.' And the 'perfect love' of Wesley's doctrine almost speaks for itself. Since the opening of the nineteenth century there have been varying approaches to the subject of this inner work of the Spirit. Anglican Evangelicalism was spiritually individualistic; then came

THE DOCTRINE OF THE HOLY SPIRIT

the other emphasis of the Oxford Movement – on the Church, baptismal regeneration, justification as a process, and the grace of the Spirit through the sacraments. There were divergences on the Continent. Schleiermacher spoke of a development within us of God-consciousness, imparted by Christ out of His own perfect God-consciousness, and developed by the Holy Spirit acting within the Church: the Holy Spirit is simply the collective spirit of the Church. Ritschl's notion of the Spirit is not unlike it, namely the motive power of the Christian community. We are reminded of F. R. Barry's judgement: 'No religion of pure immanentism can support the weight men try to make it carry' (*The Relevance of Christianity*, p. 59).

Concerning the witness of the Spirit, our final consideration, it is clear that the statement of St. Paul in Rom. viii. 16 had lost its impression some time before the history of the Early Church ended, due in no small measure to the discontinuance of the Christian prophets, the ill odour of extremist sects like the Montanists, and the strong development of hierarchical and sacramentarian ideas. When that early age passed into the medieval, Gregory the Great, in answer to an earnest inquirer, refuted any suggestion that assurance should be regarded as a normal experience; and this attitude, reinforced as time progressed by the medieval conceptions of salvation by merit and sacramental grace, was confirmed by the Council of Trent, which declared that 'no one can know, with a certainty of faith which cannot be subject to illusion, that he has obtained the grace of God'. Wyclif and Luther are both disappointing here: Wyclif said that no man, not even a pope, knows certainly 'whether he be of the Church, or whether he be a limb of the fiend' (see H. B. Workman, in *A New History of Methodism*, i., pp. 22 f.); while Luther ceased preaching assurance after coming into conflict with Protestant extremists in the sects. Calvin's doctrine of assurance, including the grace of final perseverance, referred to the elect only, as also did seventeenth-century Calvinism as expressed in the Westminster Confession. John Smith, one of the contemporary Cambridge Platonists, with a broader sympathy, spoke of the witness of the Spirit as 'a superadded taste out of God's right hand, as it were a piece of heaven in the soul, chasing away all our dark and gloomy doubtings before it' (*Select Discourses*, 449, 450). Bunyan tells how Christian at the Cross received from the third Shining One 'a mark upon his forehead' and 'a roll with a seal upon it'. This was the witness or seal of the Spirit, which the pilgrim lost and found. 'Who can tell how joyful the man was when he had gotten his roll again? For this roll was the assurance of his life, and acceptance at the desired haven. . . . Oh, how nimbly now did he go up the rest of the hill!'

John Owen's anxiety is to show that the witness is not of the *essence* of saving faith: 'It is one thing', he says, 'to have holiness really thriving in the soul, another thing for that soul to know it and to be satisfied in it; and these things may be separated.' Holiness is 'the subject of so many gospel promises' the accomplishment of which 'depends on God's faithfulness, and not on our sense of it'. But these sentiments were looked at askance by many Anglicans in the seventeenth century and by yet more in the eighteenth; we remember Bishop Butler's scepticism about 'extraordinary revelations and gifts of the Holy Ghost' which he voiced vehemently in conversation with Wesley. Barclay the Quaker definitely asserted that assurance of salvation is given in response to faith; it is 'a sensible union and friendship with God'. Wesley's father, as he lay dying, spoke to him of assurance as 'the strongest proof of Christianity', and four years afterwards his mother confessed to having this experience at the Lord's Table. Still, however, the general suspicion of such 'enthusiasm' persisted as dangerous spiritually and politically, while for many people it was a novelty, which was criticism enough. Wesley repudiated the suggestion of novelty, remarking that 'it is by God's peculiar blessing upon the

THE HOLY SPIRIT IN THE CHURCH

Methodists . . . that this great evangelical truth has been recovered, which had been for many years well-nigh lost and forgotten' (Sermon 11). It was, in his conviction, an *immediate* experience, which involved no guarantee of final perseverance but could be lost as sanctification could be lost; not of necessity connected with saving faith, but a privilege which every believer should pray for and expect to receive. How does one know a genuine case of this? Wesley answers that one knows it by the presence of humility, also by the strong proofs afforded by character: 'I lay it down as an undoubted truth, that the fruit of the Spirit is the witness of the Spirit' (Sermon 11). Further, there are the tests of the Scriptures, the testimony of our own conscience, the testimony of Christian history, consultation with other Christians, and the exercise of love in doing all possible good. Wesley's distinction between feeling and faith was as clear as Owen's; the transports of joy, which may be expected to accompany conversion, 'God sometimes giveth, sometimes withholdeth them, according to the counsels of His own will'. On the whole subject Wesley's conclusion is thus summed up by himself: '1. Let none ever presume to rest in any supposed testimony of the Spirit which is separate from the fruit of it. 2. Let none rest in any supposed fruit of the Spirit without the witness.'

The nineteenth century was a period of spiritual difficulties. Liberalism came as a revolt against a legal Deity and total depravity; inspiration was a battle-ground for contending parties; science was regarded as an enemy until some dared to speak of it as a possible friend, and in the welter many were bewildered. But it was an inevitable transition, a stirring of the Spirit amid many small and complacent things, the new reaching up through the old. We are realizing, perhaps more now than ever, that it is the Holy Spirit of God who alone can cleanse societies and remake the world; more than that, we are blind if we cannot see Him active to this end. We are also making discoveries about the structure of the human personality, and it may well be that the new science of psychology will explain, from our human end, more of how the Spirit works within us, affording release, sublimating instincts, unifying conscious and subconscious. But no man is saved *by* any human science: no human science at its best could do more than respond to the Divine Spirit. An utter surrender to the infinite power of the Spirit of God is the only way, literally, for men to take. For all human bankruptcy there is the divine wealth poured forth – from the Father and the Son through the Holy Spirit. Such is the witness of the Church through all the ages.

IV

THE HOLY SPIRIT AND THE TRINITY

by

HAROLD ROBERTS, M.A., Ph.D.

IV

THE HOLY SPIRIT AND THE TRINITY

THERE IS PROBABLY no theological doctrine which produces so much consternation and confusion in the mind of the ordinary man as the doctrine of the Trinity. It seems to bristle with inconsistencies, to create problems without solving any, and to obscure the grand simplicities of the Christian faith. The religion of Jesus, we are told, was understood by the common people since it was related to life and was completely free from the metaphysical subtleties to which theologians have devoted their mis-spent youth and maturity. If the Church is to succeed in commending the gospel to an age which, in spite of many defects, is not unsympathetic to a direct and simple appeal, it must relegate some of its teaching to the limbo of futile speculations, among which the doctrine of the Trinity will occupy the chief place.

Before we act on this advice, it may be wise to examine the grounds of the popular aversion to the doctrine. The impatient attitude which we have described sometimes extends to dogma as such. Unfortunately, the purpose of dogma is so frequently misunderstood that one almost despairs of removing the prejudices which the mere mention of the name is sufficient to arouse. It ought to be plainly stated that the function of dogma is not to eliminate mystery or to suppress intellectual inquiry or, again, to give a full exposition of the Christian faith. On the contrary, it stresses the inherent mystery of the Being and Nature of God by the exclusion of cheap solutions which would reduce Deity to the level of contemporary intelligence. Primarily, dogmas were directed against heresies which were no other than false simplifications of the divine revelation. They were not intended to suppress freedom of thought but to mark out the territory within which freedom could be fruitfully exercised. While they do not provide an intellectual explanation of Christianity, they do state as firmly as human language may the facts which are to be explained. Since dogma claims to be the expression of truth, and nothing but truth, it is inevitable that it should share the exclusiveness that characterizes truth in all its phases.

It would not, however, be fair to suggest that the antipathy towards the doctrine of the Trinity is entirely due to a distaste for dogma. Allowance

THE HOLY SPIRIT AND THE TRINITY

must be made for the fact that the orthodox formulae do not make easy reading; and we cannot but admit that the attempts of theologians, ancient and modern, to interpret their meaning have been singularly disappointing. As the medical profession puts it, the treatment is not satisfactory or the patient does not respond to treatment. It is the latter phrase that theologians would prefer to borrow, but the former more accurately describes the situation. In view of the fact that the personality of the Divine Being is unique in the sense that it belongs to an order other than human, it is unavoidable that any attempt to wrest its secret should fail. Human analogies misrepresent almost as much as they represent the nature of God, and, when we take into account the difficulties relating to the psychology of human personality, our judgement upon the history of the doctrine of the Trinity should at least be tempered with mercy. On the other hand, it is greatly to be desired that theologians in larger numbers should direct their attention to the importance of this doctrine and draw out its implications for worship, thought, and conduct. If the theologian is faithful to his task, which is to interpret the content of the Christian Revelation of God in the light of the growing experience of the Church and not simply to examine archaeological remains, he will find

THE DOCTRINE OF THE HOLY SPIRIT

that the doctrine of the Trinity makes his theology truly systematic and provides the only adequate basis for the life of devotion and service. While, as theologian, he is not concerned with the philosophical implications of this doctrine, he will not be slow to perceive that he is in possession of a principle of interpretation that enables him to make sense of reality as a whole.

These positions we shall endeavour to maintain in the sequel. First of all, we must consider the meaning and origin of the doctrine of the Trinity.

I

The Eastern and Western Churches each used a different formula to express the content of the Christian belief about God, and, unfortunately, it is not possible to discover the precise meaning of the words employed in either formula. In the Eastern Church, the statement which received official recognition was 'One essence (*ousia*) in three hypostases'. The Latins, following Tertullian, spoke of 'One substance in three persons'. Many difficult questions might be raised at this point, but we shall confine our attention to one of them. Both formulae are agreed as to the unity of the Godhead and unequivocally affirm it. Hence the use of the term *ousia* with the Latin *substantia* as its practical equivalent. The word *persona*, however, is not a synonym for 'hypostasis' as used

THE HOLY SPIRIT AND THE TRINITY

by the Cappadocians, who played an important part in the formulation of the doctrine of the Trinity, nor does it correspond to the modern meaning of personality. Up to the Council of Nicea in A.D. 325 *ousia* and 'hypostasis' have the same meaning, but at the Synod of Alexandria in A.D. 362 recognition was given to the word 'hypostasis' and it was employed in the sense of the Latin *persona*. Now, *persona* meant, not an individual centre of consciousness, but a *rôle* or character, as in the title *dramatis personae*. While the status or function assumed is not regarded as something apart from an individual agent, the emphasis is on the part played by an individual in any given circumstances rather than upon his existence as a separate subject.

The Cappadocians, however, particularly Basil of Caesarea, gave to 'hypostasis' something approaching the modern meaning of personality. 'Not the indefinite conception of *ousia*', writes Basil,[1] 'which, because what is signified is common to all, finds no fixity, but that which by means of the special characteristics (or properties) which are made apparent, gives fixity and circumspection to that which is common and uncircumscribed.' He further explains that *ousia* is related to 'hypostasis' in the same way as the common is related to the particular. 'Every one of us both shares in

[1] Ep. 38. 214.

existence by the common term of *ousia*, and by his own properties is such or such an one. In the same manner in the matter in question the term *ousia* is common, like goodness or Godhead or any similar attribute (i.e. it is not goodness or Godhead or any attribute); while "hypostasis" is contemplated in the property of Fatherhood, Sonship, or the power to sanctify.' That is to say, Dr. Bethune-Baker[1] remarks, after quoting these passages in a valuable note on *ousia*-hypostasis, 'hypostasis expresses the particular mode of existence or special function. The one Being exists in three forms or spheres or functions. The one God is tri-personal'. We would submit, however, that the terms 'forms' or 'spheres' or 'functions' do not adequately represent Basil's meaning. It is clear from his conception of *ousia* as something indefinite, and as bearing the same relation to 'hypostasis' as the common to the particular, that by 'hypostasis' he means a concrete individual, and his use of the term comes nearer to the modern significance of person than to the Latin word *persona*. Further confirmation of this interpretation is found in his comparison of the Three Persons to Paul, Silas, and Timothy.

It is difficult, indeed, to absolve the Cappadocians from the charge of harbouring the tritheistic tendencies so often condemned and embraced by

[1] *An Introduction to the Early History of Christian Doctrine*, p. 238.

one and the same theologian in our own day. That these tendencies are not to be regarded as a legitimate development of the Patristic doctrine of the Trinity is borne out by the similes used by the Old Nicenes – the sun, its rays, the river, the tree, the branch – and it is plain that they cannot be reconciled with the adumbration of the doctrine which we find in St. Augustine and Aquinas. St. Augustine speaks of the persons of the Trinity as Power, Wisdom, Love. Most of his analogies are psychological – memory, understanding, will; the object seen, the act of seeing, the attention of the mind. It is to the mind of man in its highest phases that he looks for light on the mystery of the Trinity, since man has been made in the image of God; but the trinities which he traces in human experience are indicative, not of tritheism, but of a single consciousness in which three distinctive activities or functions have their ground.

St. Thomas, again, speaks of God as at one and the same time Power, Wisdom, and Will (or Love, since the operation of the divine will is inseparable from love). It is interesting to notice that both St. Thomas and St. Augustine hold that the love of the Father for the Son is the Holy Spirit. The relation of love, however, between the Father and the Son cannot be described as a person in the modern sense of the

THE DOCTRINE OF THE HOLY SPIRIT

term. Dr. W. R. Matthews,[1] while fully recognizing that this interpretation as it stands is unsatisfactory, for it presupposes that the relation between two terms is itself a term, suggests as an alternative that the relation between the Father and the Son gives rise (not temporally) to the being of the Holy Spirit. With due caution he appeals to the analogy of the social mind. 'If then there is in the very imperfect societies known to us something which, transcending all individuals taken singly, can be called even metaphorically a social mind, we might expect that this characteristic would be perfectly developed in a perfect society. Perhaps that would mean that, in this instance alone, the social mind would have passed beyond all metaphor and be real mind – fully personal will and intelligence. This speculation may be accepted for what it is worth. I do not claim more for it than that it indicates the possibility that in the case of the Godhead the relation between the First and Second Persons may itself be personal.'[2] The author does not advance this theory with any great confidence, and we are not altogether surprised. Apart from the fact that it is dangerous to use an analogy that may in itself be nothing more than a metaphor, it is still difficult to understand how the relation

[1] *God in Christian Thought and Experience*, pp. 195–8.
[2] Op. cit., p. 198.

THE HOLY SPIRIT AND THE TRINITY

between Father and Son can give rise to the Holy Spirit as a Being with whom we may have personal relations.[1] And, in any case, we are left with a tritheistic doctrine on our hands.

It is plain that the Church in its Trinitarian teaching has sought to steer a middle course between tritheism and the Sabellian view which severs the distinctions in the Godhead from their basis in the eternal nature of God. The distinctions, that is, were merely temporary or phenomenal phases in the life of God whose real Being is unknown to us. Unfortunately, the terminology available in the early centuries was highly ambiguous, and had it been possible to find terms that safeguarded the unity of the Godhead without surrendering the distinctive characteristics of its activities in creation, redemption, and inspiration, much confusion might have been avoided. It cannot, of course, be said that we are to-day in possession of a satisfactory terminology, but certainly we can no longer avail ourselves of the concepts of 'substance' and 'hypostasis', not only because we have rightly ceased to employ them in philosophic thought, but because they yield a conception of God which is other than Christian. On the other hand, it is

---

[1] Op. cit., p. 188. 'The doctrine of the Trinity does mean to assert that there are three distinct Beings within the Godhead, with each of whom personal relations on the part of man are possible.'

necessary to conserve the values which those who used these categories sought to express. With that end in view, some writers make use of the term 'centre', and, while it has the merits of a convenient vagueness, it is open to many objections. To speak of 'three centres of one consciousness' (Temple)[1] or 'three centres of one activity' (A. E. Taylor)[2] is tantamount to tritheism. One consciousness can only have one centre in the ontological sense, although it may have many centres of interest; and it is difficult to see how one activity can have three centres (in the former sense) other than in a society of three individual beings.

The attempts to interpret the doctrine of the Trinity by reference to the analogy of society – not necessarily the group mind – in which unity and multiplicity are perfectly reconciled, point, not to the Catholic doctrine, but to Pluralism. Dr. Tennant, in his book on *Philosophical Theology*,[3] expounds without advocating the social interpretation, and his statement may be briefly summarized. Human beings owe their pre-eminence over lower forms of life to their capacity for social organization into over-individual unities which are not merely aggregates of individuals. The principle of

[1] *Christus Veritas*, p. 117.
[2] *Essays, Catholic and Critical*, p. 140 (quoted).
[3] pp. 170–2.

continuity points to the possibility that individuals of a higher order are similarly organized into over-individual unities – it may be *ad indefinitum*. This view suggests that a society rather than an individual is the highest form of unity. The divine persons who constitute the supreme unity may be regarded as less individual than human persons. A divine person is conceivably free from those limitations which prevent our knowing directly the states of another. The unity may be so close that each may be directly concerned in the activities of the other, and the idea of 'perichoresis', or mutual penetration, may be applied literally to persons in a perfect society. Whatever speculative value this theory may possess – and we are not at present concerned with speculation – it is but remotely connected with the Christian doctrine of the Trinity. It is sufficient to say with Dr. Tennant that 'the recent tendency of orthodox theologians to speak of God as "a social being", and to appropriate such philosophical advantages as the conception of a plural Deity would offer, involves an unconscious desertion of the Catholic faith'.[1]

We should be well advised, in our endeavour to restate the doctrine of the Trinity, to avoid the superficial attractions of a formula which is necessarily abstract, and for that reason misleading,

[1] Op. cit., pp. 268–9.

and to content ourselves with affirmations which, if lacking in conciseness, yet take account of the richness of the Christian revelation of God. While recognizing that the nature of God defies verbal expression, we can affirm that the life of God is personal and that it constitutes a unity. The Divine Nature has been made known to us in three activities which are not of accidental or temporary significance, but which derive from Its character as Eternal Love. These activities we may describe as creation, redemption, and inspiration, and, although they are distinctive in nature, they proceed from one and the same Being and are controlled by one and the same purpose. It is the Eternal Love of God that brought the world into existence, that offers itself for our redemption in the historic person of Jesus Christ, and that energizes within us so that we may respond to its holy appeal. Within each activity God Himself is to be found. The Creator of the world is none other than its Redeemer, none other than He who brings order out of chaos and by the inspiration of His own spirit banishes the night of darkness and sin. In this sense, which preserves the fundamental intention of the Catholic Faith, we may with gladness declare, 'We worship one God in Trinity and Trinity in Unity'.

THE HOLY SPIRIT AND THE TRINITY

II

The significance of the doctrine of the Trinity will be more fully apprehended if we consider its relation to Christian experience. It was the recognition, by the Church, of Christ as divine, that necessitated the formulation of the belief in the Trinity. The attempts to find the source of the doctrine in the One, the Reason, and the World-Soul of Neo-Platonism – a trinity whose members are not co-equal – or in the triads of pagan religions may be said to have completely failed.[1] Further, while the doctrine does not conflict with the religion of the Old Testament, it cannot be doubted that the stern monotheism of Judaism hindered rather than precipitated its acceptance. There is no tenable explanation of the rise of Trinitarianism other than the determination to hold together the belief in the divinity of Christ, the unity of God, and the existence of the Christian community. The doctrine of the Trinity was not the outcome of idle or serious speculation; on the contrary, it was the fruit of a lofty endeavour to do justice to the elements in the experience of the Christian Church which were held to be vital to the faith. What were those elements?

[1] Cf. the important essay by K. E. Kirk, 'The Evolution of the Doctrine of the Trinity', in *Essays on the Trinity and the Incarnation* (ed. by Rawlinson).

THE DOCTRINE OF THE HOLY SPIRIT

The Old Testament conception of God as living, holy, and personal, as sovereign Lord of creation, was presupposed in Apostolic Christianity, as indeed by our Lord Himself. The Apostles, however, without surrendering or even compromising their belief in the unity of God, began to make their crucified, risen, and ascended Lord the object of adoration. It would appear that they could not think of God without the thought of Christ occupying a central place in their mind. While they were unable to explain the relation existing between Christ and God, they were not thereby discouraged from offering to Christ the worship formerly reserved for God alone. Christ had for them, in the famous but equivocal phrase, the 'value of God' and the dogma of His divinity, when it came to be formulated, expressed the conviction which is enshrined in the New Testament that no one can have the value of God unless he is divine.

Those who responded to the love of God, as it was revealed in the life and passion of our Lord, and in the miracle of His resurrection, became conscious of a power that took possession of their whole being. They were brought into a new relationship with God, whom they called 'Abba, Father' – a term which signified the intimacy of the new life in God which they now enjoyed. While in the Old Testament the idea of the

Fatherhood of God is represented, it is conceived within the framework of Kingship, and God is regarded mainly as a King who issues commands rather than as a Father who welcomes sinners to the inner circle of His home. The Christian believers, however, are no longer slaves, but sons, and the freedom of sons is theirs. Through their dependence upon God in Christ they are free to think, to worship, and to serve. Their thinking is governed by an unchanging standard – the mind of Christ – and the worship they offer is bound by nothing save the restraints of love. In the service of their heavenly Father they find that perfect liberty that comes of a deliverance from the bondage of self-centredness and of a consciousness of a debt of gratitude that can never be repaid.

Again, they became united in a fellowship which they did not create, but found. Barriers of race, sex, and class were broken down, and differences served to deepen the unity of the fellowship rather than to disturb its peace. In that fellowship they began to grow in the knowledge of God and to manifest in their lives the unsearchable riches of His grace. It is this power, liberated through the human response to the divine revelation in Christ, that the New Testament describes as Holy Spirit. The Spirit of God, it is true, is to be seen at work in creation and in the hearts of men everywhere. The impulse that lies

THE DOCTRINE OF THE HOLY SPIRIT

behind scientific and artistic achievement, or that prompts any act of self-sacrifice, is itself the activity of the Holy Spirit. Nevertheless, although the doctrine of the Holy Spirit in New Testament writings does not exclude what is generally described as the immanence of God, since wherever love, joy, peace, kindliness, and fidelity are found, there the presence of the Spirit is to be discerned, it is important to notice that in the experience of the Early Church the Holy Spirit is the name given to the peculiar influence that took possession of those who answered the love of God displayed in Jesus Christ with the dedication of their lives.

While Trinitarianism in its developed form is not to be found in the New Testament, and while it is not easy to determine the particular status that is assigned to the Holy Spirit in His relation to the Father and the Son, the experience of God enshrined within its pages constitutes plainly enough the source and justification of the Catholic doctrine of the Trinity. There we find an attempt which bears the marks, not of dialectical skill, but of an irrepressible experience, to hold together the belief in God as the Creator of the world, perfect in holiness and infinite in power, as the Saviour of men who shared man's sorrow and bore the burden of his sin, as the Spirit who energizes and agonizes in the world of Nature and in the human soul, kindling a desire to respond to the Revelation of God in Jesus Christ and binding those who yield to His appeal into a living fellowship. God is Love, and the mystery of His Love has been manifested in the threefold revelation of Himself as Father, Son, and Holy Spirit. Here we have the sanction of Trinitarian theology, and no conception of God, which means less than that the Divine Nature has been made known through three permanent determinations or functions of His being, can be regarded as in harmony with the record of the experience of the Christian Community embedded in the New Testament and the historic creeds.

III

In conclusion, let us consider the value of the doctrine of the Trinity for philosophy and religion. Among modern philosophers, those who do not despair of discovering a meaning in Reality as a whole, and who acknowledge the objectivity or validity of moral and spiritual values, accept with few exceptions the theistic view which maintains that the ground of the universe is a Supreme Being least inadequately described as personal, in whom perfect power is combined with perfect goodness.[1] What we wish

[1] Cf. art. 'Theism' by A. E. Taylor in *Encyclopaedia of Religion and Ethics*.

THE DOCTRINE OF THE HOLY SPIRIT

to suggest is that theism finds in the doctrine of the Trinity its logical completion. If the ultimate Reality is perfect love, as a theist is compelled to hold, the divine activities represented in Trinitarian theology are such as might reasonably be inferred from the nature of love. It is of the essence of love to reveal itself and to share its life with another. It cannot rest until its secret is unveiled. Divine love, however, can only be perfectly manifested in One who is Himself divine, and who by reason of His being and character is able to mediate that love to men. The absence of the Incarnation would constitute the major difficulty of theism, since it would point to a defect in either the love or the power of God. But not even the revelation of divine love is sufficient to secure a response from free beings. Unless the transcendent God is active within the human heart, so that the desire for goodness may triumph over the stubbornness of the will and its environment, the purpose of love cannot be fulfilled. Hence we would submit that just as the recognition of the objectivity of values leads inevitably to theism, so the full acceptance of theistic implications necessitates the belief in God the Father, God the Son, and God the Holy Ghost, One God, revealed in the three activities of His Being.

We have already referred to the apparent

disparity between the Trinitarian formula – one God in three persons – and the requirements of the religious life. It is our conviction, however, that nothing short of the doctrine of the Trinity is adequate to the devotional and practical needs of the Christian believer. The relevance of the doctrine is perceived when we consider the importance of cultivating an experience of God that does justice to all the revealed aspects of His Being. If we concentrate our attention on God the Father to the exclusion of God the Son and God the Holy Spirit, we inevitably begin to despair of ever keeping His laws, and a religion of grace is converted into a monotonous experience of frustrated effort. To equate Christianity with the belief in the Fatherhood of God, in the supposed interests of a simple faith, is to neglect the sanction of that belief, which is God's action in Christ, and to surrender the hope of our ever being able to know God as our Father. 'The Spirit Himself beareth witness unto our spirit that we are the children of God' (Rom. viii. 16). If, again, we worship the Son to the exclusion of the Father and the Spirit, we relapse into a pernicious form of ditheism which converts the Father into a Being whom nobody knows or wants to know. The door is also opened to a dangerous preoccupation with the Jesus of history, which results in the attempted suppression of ultimate questions and in the facile humanistic assumption that a vision of His beauty, heroism, and love will suffice to cleanse our hearts from every selfish stain and to assure us of His divinity. We cannot, however, indefinitely postpone ultimate questions, as the Church itself soon discovered, and it is certainly undesirable that we should even make the attempt. If Jesus Christ was not Very God of very God, Christianity loses its uniqueness and at once forfeits the claim to be the religion for all mankind. Further, it is not simply by the unaided exercise of our own insight that we come to acknowledge the divinity of our Lord. The Spirit of God working within us disposes us to recognize that which is akin to Himself, and to respond to it. 'No man can say, Jesus is Lord, but in the Holy Spirit' (1 Cor. xii. 3).

Finally, if we exclude the first and second persons of the Trinity and worship the Holy Spirit alone, our religion will deteriorate into that kind of immanentism which finds God everywhere in general but nowhere in particular. Also, the distinction between our own spirit and the Holy Spirit will become blurred, and the assurance of the validity of such guidance as we receive will not be forthcoming since we have virtually abandoned our standard of reference, which is the Mind of Christ. It is imperative that

THE HOLY SPIRIT AND THE TRINITY

we should keep before us in our thought and devotion the affirmation contained in the Nicene Creed: 'who proceedeth from the Father and the Son.' That is, the world from the beginning has been fashioned by the Spirit of God the Father Almighty. It is His Spirit that lies behind the mysterious beauty of Nature, the achievements of poet and prophet, and the onward march of humanity towards its predestined goal. The nature of the goal and the way to it have been disclosed in the life and work of Jesus Christ. In Him the Spirit's power was manifested with a new fullness. It was none other than the Spirit of God the Father Almighty that was incarnate in our Lord, since the God of Creation and of redemption are one and the same. But, as we have seen, fresh resources and opportunities were liberated by the coming of our Lord and by the consummation of His life in the Cross and the Resurrection. The promise contained in the words 'He shall take of mine and show it unto you' was abundantly fulfilled. The Spirit, that is, presents to man the nature of his destiny as revealed in Christ, and kindles within him a desire to make a glad and unqualified response. He does not, however, leave him, once the response has been made. He energizes within the soul and within its world until every impulse is subdued and every desire is brought into perfect harmony with divine love. 'I believe in the Holy Ghost, the Lord and Giver of life, who proceedeth from the Father and the Son.'

In our worship and in the practice of the Christian life we need to embrace the whole faith, for it is the whole faith, and not a garbled selection, that saves. We are bidden by St. Paul to put on the whole armour of God, and what is that but God in the fullness and richness of His being, Father, Son, and Holy Spirit? To the Triune Name alone is the glory due, now and always.

www.ingramcontent.com/pod-product-compliance
Lightning Source LLC
Chambersburg PA
CBHW050837160426
43192CB00011B/2055